Cultural Interactions in Europe and the Eastern Mediterranean during the Bronze Age (3000-500 BC)

Papers from a session held at the European Association of Archaeologists Sixth Annual Meeting in Lisbon 2000

Edited by

Bozena Werbart

BAR International Series 985
2001

Published in 2016 by
BAR Publishing, Oxford

BAR International Series 985

Cultural Interactions in Europe and the Eastern Mediterranean during the Bronze Age (3000–500 BC)

© The editors and contributors severally and the Publisher 2001

The authors' moral rights under the 1988 UK Copyright,
Designs and Patents Act are hereby expressly asserted.

All rights reserved. No part of this work may be copied, reproduced, stored,
sold, distributed, scanned, saved in any form of digital format or transmitted
in any form digitally, without the written permission of the Publisher.

ISBN 9781841712710 paperback
ISBN 9781407353371 e-format
DOI https://doi.org/10.30861/9781841712710
A catalogue record for this book is available from the British Library

BAR Publishing is the trading name of British Archaeological Reports (Oxford) Ltd.
British Archaeological Reports was first incorporated in 1974 to publish the BAR
Series, International and British. In 1992 Hadrian Books Ltd became part of the BAR
group. This volume was originally published by Archaeopress in conjunction with
British Archaeological Reports (Oxford) Ltd / Hadrian Books Ltd, the Series principal
publisher, in 2001. This present volume is published by BAR Publishing, 2016.

BAR
PUBLISHING

BAR titles are available from:

        BAR Publishing
        122 Banbury Rd, Oxford, OX2 7BP, UK
EMAIL   info@barpublishing.com
PHONE +44 (0)1865 310431
FAX   +44 (0)1865 316916
        www.barpublishing.com

Contents

Bozena Werbart
Introduction: Cultural interactions in Europe and the eastern Mediterranean
during the Bronze Age (3000-500 BC) 1

Amnon Ben-Tor
Hazor – the rise and fall of the "Head of all those Kingdoms" 7

Li Winter
Cultural encounters
Symbols from the Mediterranean world in the South Scandinavian rock carving tradition
during the Bronze Age 9

Eva Hjärthner-Holdar & Christina Risberg
The innovation of iron
From Bronze Age to Iron Age societies in Sweden and Greece 29

Luiz Oosterbeek
Diffusion, dissemination and interaction
The contradictions of past realities or of present perspectives 43

Göran Burenhult
Long-distance cultural interaction in megalithic Europe:
Carrowmore and the Irish megalithic tradition in a western European and Mediterranean context 47

Amanda-Alice Maravelia
Sapho's poetry and ancient Egyptian love poems: a field of comparative interpretation 67

Authors & addresses

Ben-Tor, Amnon. Institute of Archaeology, Hebrew University of Jerusalem, 91905 Jerusalem, Israel
Email: bentor@h2.hum.huji.ac.il

Burenhult, Göran. Gotland University College, Cramergatan 3, 621 57 Visby, Sweden.
Email: burenhult@hgo.se

Hjärthner-Holdar, Eva. Geoarchaeological Laboratory, Swedish National Heritage Board, Uppsala, Sweden.
Email: eva.hjarthner_holdar@raa.se

Maravelia, Amanda-Alice. Centre de Recherches en Sciences de l'Antiquité, Faculté des Lettres et des Sciences Humaines, Université de Limoges. 39E, Rue Camille Guérin, F 87036, Limoges Cedex. France.
& P.O. Box 70330. GR-16601, Glyphada, Athens, Greece.
Email: <nut_ntrt@otenet.gr

Winter, Li. Department of Archaeology, University of Stockholm
106 91 Stockholm, Sweden
Email: liwinter72@hotmail.com

Oosterbeek, Luiz. Centro de Pré-História do Instituto Politécnico de Tomar, Estrada da Serra, 2300 Tomar, Portugal
Email: loost@ipt.pt

Risberg, Christina. Department of Archaeology and Ancient History, University of Uppsala, 753 10 Uppsala, Sweden.
Email: christina.risberg@antiken.uu.se

Werbart, Bozena. Institute of Archaeology and Sami studies, Umeå University, 901 87 Umeå, Sweden
Email: bozena.werbart@arke.umu.e

Introduction: Cultural Interactions in Europe and the Eastern Mediterranean during the Bronze Age (3000-500 BC)

Bozena Werbart

Cultural Interactions in Europe and the Eastern Mediterranean during the Bronze Age was the title of the session on EAA2000 6th Annual Meeting in Lisbon 2000. The main issue is cultural interactionism in the Mediterranean World and Temperate Europe 3000-500 BC.

Any attempt to understand present-day European societies and a possible "European identity" must include a historical perspective. Many of the phenomena on the road from the Stone Age to urbanization and the "Cities of tomorrow" affecting Europe and its development between c. 3000 and 500 BC appeared first in southeastern Mediterranean Europe (in the Aegean area), influenced by the cultures in the Eastern Mediterranean such as Anatolia, Egypt and the Levant either directly or indirectly. These phenomena gradually spread through all of Europe.

The important issue is to focus on how these impulses were transmitted, what forms of interaction led to their spread and acceptance, and why certain societies did not accept them. Important issues are also how these impulses affected cultural identity and changes in social structures. By studying the development of the European continent (and its relation to the rest of the Eastern Mediterranean area) from 3000 to 500 BC, we hope to be able to determine some of the underlying causes and results of cultural interactions, transmissions, changes, diversities, and transformations on various facets of the societies. In other words, which innovations were transmitted and which were not, how they were transmitted, the kind of interactions (economic, religious/symbolic, political, military, social) which permitted the spread of these innovations, and the results in and for the receiver society.

Although European societies seem to have evolved largely independently for some three millennia after the initiation of agriculture, the continent was not isolated from what was happening in the nuclear area of the Eastern Mediterranean.

The effects of Near East urbanization socially, ecologically, economically and ideologically slowly but fundamentally transformed the situation in Temperate Europe.

Urbanization involved fundamental changes in the nature of material culture, because it was essentially an asymmetric set of exchanges of manufactured products for raw materials. It therefore created and disseminated a whole range of new, artificial materials and manufacturing processes, especially in the media of display – food, eating/drinking equipment, furniture, textiles, ornaments, weapons, means of transport. Many of these specialized crafts remained confined to palace centers with resources and special expertise. The spread of drinking habits, modes of clothing, metallurgical technologies, vehicle use, new types of furniture, etc., all brought a new range of products to consume, and to trade in. They therefore slowly transformed the economic and social potentials not only of the core/periphery area but the margin as well (Sherratt 1993). The effects on Temperate Europe of the new wave of innovations started by Near Eastern urbanization via the south-east Mediterranean area can thus be separated into two phases: a phase from c. 3000 to 2000 BC in which the absorption of a variety of new elements began to diversify production; and a phase of faster development which began around 2000 BC, in which the adoption of bronze and the emergence of standard categories of artifacts began to articulate regional specialization through a common language of consumption and medium of exchange.

Bronze Age Temperate Europe was linked to the contemporary Mediterranean world as the result of contacts and interactions. Contacts between Bronze Age Temperate Europe and the contemporary Mediterranean world reached deep into the continent, and were also significant for Mediterranean societies themselves. The important centres of the Mediterranean world – Mycenae, Crete, Troy, and Etruria – spread their culture and influence when northern feeder routes entered the arteries of maritime trade, which connected the urban world. Although islands such as Cyprus, Crete, and Sardinia played a crucial role in the westward spread of urban systems, long-term growth was concentrated in areas, which had a continental hinterland. The marginal routes created by successive phases of westward expansion – along the Danube and Black Sea, across the Alps, and later west to Spain/Portugal – were vital in determining the future expansion of the great centres of Mediterranean civilization. Particularly significant for future developments was the formation around 1600 BC of the direct route between the Baltic and the Mediterranean: the corridor canonized in older generation of textbooks as the "amber route": exchanges of inter- and transcontinental proportions. This route was an important precursor of the structures underlying the later development of European polities (Sherratt 1993).

How were these innovations and impulses transmitted? What forms of interaction (social, economic, religious, and military) led to their spread and acceptance, or lack thereof? What are the mechanisms behind transformation on various levels? Can abstract, symbolic beliefs be transferred? Can the adoption of certain abstract, symbolic values cause specific and similar changes in social structure? How do such changes affect cultural identity and concept of self? Does the general spread and acceptance of a common set of phenomena lead to a common result in all cases? If not, why not? These are some of the questions about the past which must be dealt with before ever achieving an understanding of the present.

Four major aspects of human development are therefore very important:

> *Invention, technology and craft specialization*
> adoption/rejection of various technologies, results of this choice for the various societies, diffusion patterns
>
> *Cultural identity*
> as seen in the material record, iconography and social organization
>
> *Communication*
> which includes two major fields: symbolic and abstract, including religion/rites, and trade, exchange, and contact.
>
> *Social transformation*
> focused on local, regional and international levels and related to different contexts and landscapes. The role of urbanization and its effects on social life will also be studied.

Invention, technology and craft specialization

Invention, technology and craft specialization in the past influenced of course the contemporary European societies. Adoption/rejection of various technologies, results of this choice for the various societies, and diffusion patterns are issues of the past, the present, and the future. Although most of the innovations came to Europe via Greece, their spread in area and in time and their acceptance or rejection in the rest of Europe varied far more than the linear distance from the source. For example, by c. 3000 BC. or a little before, copper technology in Greece was well developed, and alloys of copper and other metals/minerals (bronze) were in common use after only some few hundred years. Bronze technology didn't reach Scandinavia, for example, until roughly 1000 years later. Iron, however, which was first in use in Greece in the 11th/10th c., was already a feature of daily life in northern Europe in the 5th/4th c. (Gillis 1999; Gillis 2000 *in print*). On the other hand, the rise of urbanization and cities is commonly dated to c. 700 BC. or shortly before in Greece, while cities do not appear in northern Europe for at least 1500 years.

One area of particular interest in the transmission of innovations is that of metallurgy and metal production, and the role of economics (trade and/or contacts) as opposed to (or in conjunction with) that of social constructions (development of an elite, gift exchange, etc.) in this transmission.

Metallurgy in early Iron Age Greece was diffused throughout Europe both from and to the East/West-North/South. The Nordic metal smiths was inspired to experiment with new motifs, which existed on imported items from Central and South East Europe and from the Mycenaean world. Thus, although bronze appeared first in an Aegean context, copper and metallurgy in general has a much older background and history in central and southeastern Europe. As mentioned above, some issues which need to be determined in this context are whether the spread of metal knowledge and technology at the end of the 4th millennium came to central and southeastern Europe directly from the Near East or whether the development in central and southeastern Europe was indigenous. Further, this raises the question of from where the Aegean area received the impulse – the Near East directly, or from the areas immediately to the north of the Aegean, i.e., the Balkans and Central Europe, or even an innovation which arose with no outside influence. In any case, before an understanding of the spread of metallurgical innovation can be understood in a European context, the background and origins should be clarified.

Naturally the transmission of metallurgy implies much more and affects many aspects of the societies. A study of the effects of the adoption of this technology implies also studies of the socio-economic, political and religious structures of each society as the innovation spreads. What effect did metal technology have on the rise of elites and in specific warrior elités, entrepreneurship or other, trade, state formation, and much more?

In the long run, such a study can give information about social-economic developments, which may be common to several or all societies in Europe.

Cultural identity

The role of archaeology in construction and legitimizing of collective identities is one of the most important questions in archaeological theory and practice. Cultural identity in archaeology can be interpreted as a conglomerate of different cultural manifestations in different societies. Cultural identity is a flexible and subjective phenomenon, it is a process: societies can change identities, and can identify themselves with different groups of people and societies. Interactions with other groups can influence the group's own cultural identity. Cultural identity can, therefore, be seen as a social, diversified and dynamic phenomenon, which can be (and often is) affected and altered by social and cultural interactions (Werbart 1996; Werbart 1997).

Cultural changes, in as much as they can be read from the archaeological record, are primarily a factor of movement of people, migration or colonization. The close relationship of artefacts, material culture and cultural identity in this context is considered, of course, self-evident. However, it is not fixed and stable features, such as dress, material culture or language, which identify a group, but its boundaries separating from other groups, as well as the maintenance of these flexible boundaries which form its distinctive character. Globalism, pluralism and the potentials of the past are a common denominator in studies of human changes and cultural identities. One of the regions of archaeology, Middle East and Eastern Mediterranean will be seen in this project from a global view, an extra-European perspective. With the positive view of the future - with development of international and transnational scientific co-operations, secularization of daily lives and real pluralism – "archaeology itself may no longer be able to be claimed as *any* scholar's game" (Silberman 1998:186).

The region of Mediterranean and Middle East played historically on the one hand a fundamental role in the archaeology's birth; on the other hand this area was often ignored (Bernal 1987; Kostakis 1998; Werbart 2000). Discourses about cultural identity are characterized not only by globalism, but also by nostalgia, a fascination with the exotic and exoticness of the Other.

Any debates on the socio-politics of the past in the Middle East and Eastern Mediterranean is an intellectualization, a construction - the "Orient" has been constructed as the Other of Europe. And with the globalization of Others as a result of mobility, migrations and tourism, the "Otherness" has been domesticated. In the current transition to globalism, we must also understand cultural identity as a identity within a specific socio-political context of "memorabilia" (the role of objects of cultural heritage in cultural memory), and the role of archaeological monuments, ruins, relics etc. in the dynamics of self-identity and group affiliation.

Cultural interactionism in the Mediterranean World and in the Temperate Europe is seen in the archaeological record, i.a. by prehistoric material culture, changes in the use of landscape, settlement patterns and urbanization. The relevance of these important events in the past are of great importance to modern societies, because the past problems (urbanization, minorities, cultural diversities, and the preservations of cultural heritage) must be dealt with before ever achieving an understanding of the present.

The Eastern Mediterranean world, a key area between Europe and Asia, in many situations influenced cultural inter-contacts and meetings between different peoples, societies and *modus vivendi* (see Ben-Tor in this volume). Despite the geographical location of the area in question, which was often responsible for personal and ethnic tragedies, the constructive and stimulating role of this region (of different cultures and peoples) cannot be neglected. This role influenced the character of later European cultures and later European history.

Communication
Communication, one of the four major aspects of human behavior to be studied here and one of the important factors in the past, is of great relevance and of vital significance for contemporary societies. Communication includes two major fields: symbolic and abstract, including religion/rites, and trade, exchange, and contact. Symbolic or abstract communication concerns the transmission of symbols, ideas and conceptions through Bronze Age Europe, and how different ritual practices and beliefs were introduced and adopted in many parts of Europe through various forms of human interaction and exchange systems. The project "Mediterranean symbols in the South Scandinavian rock-carving tradition during the Bronze Age" (see Winter in this volume) concern the appearance of certain symbols and symbolic structures in the rock-carving tradition and the material culture from the South Scandinavian Bronze Age which can be related to the eastern Mediterranean area. The fact that there are certain symbols and also objects in southern Scandinavia with parallels in the eastern Mediterranean cultures show that there were connections and trading networks in Europe and the Mediterranean during the Bronze Age, and it is important to try to illuminate this interaction and transformation. The study is based on an interdisciplinary analysis of the use of symbols in the South Scandinavian Bronze Age in a broad European perspective, combining Nordic archaeology, classical archaeology and history (Olsson 1999).

Throughout the prehistory of Europe a relatively extensive transmission of symbols and related material culture took place. Did new religious beliefs and mentalities follow the transmission over large areas, and did the function and meaning of the symbols change in a different social context? Studies of the central European material are essentially important, due to the fact that the area represent the geographic "bridge" between areas that are separated both culturally and geographically. It is important to include Central Europe and the Carpathian Basin in these discussions, due to the fact that this region had a very special status during the EBA. A new social structure seems to appear already at the end of the later Neolithic period and can be seen in terms of chiefdoms, a more differentiated society, and an increase in trade and exchange. From ca 1700 BC, Central Europe and the Unêtice culture were the main areas for contacts with both Scandinavia and the Eastern Mediterranean. As a result of the increasing trade and exchange between Scandinavia and continental Europe, many southern elements found in new items, technology and in the art and decoration came to be integrated into the Scandinavian Bronze Age cultures. This influence can of course also be seen in records from religious and ritual activities. Several aspects of human behavior show many similarities between North, Central and southeastern Europe. The Adriatic coast, with a key position on the sea-routes linking the Balkan region to the Italian heel and the northern Adriatic to the Aegean world had good natural routes leading to other parts of the Balkan region. It can be expected that this area experienced many different cultural influences and interactions.

The especially important research questions are:

*The presence/existence of various symbols in Central

Europe – similarities/differences and contacts with southern Scandinavia and the eastern Mediterranean.

*Symbolic transmission and social transformation in Bronze Age Europe and the Eastern Mediterranean.

*The transmission of a élite ideology in Europe and the Near East in the second millennium BC.

*Symbols in a Bronze Age cosmogony: eastern Mediterranean and Scandinavia (Larsson 1997; Larsson 1999).

Social transformation
One of the most important aspects of every culture seems to be the way human beings try to change their environment in order to achieve more safe conditions of their lives, better access to natural resources, better political and social standing. The Helladic world in Greece (ca.2100-1050 BC) was a culture of settled societies who lived mostly in towns and smaller settlements and villages (Lewartowski 1995). The study of the development, similarities, diversities and changes of human settlements is thus the study of social transformation.

Social transformation studied in local, regional and international levels are related to different contexts: the movement of objects, ideas, impulses and symbols from and even to Greece and the Aegean up through the rest of Europe between 3000-500 BC. The effects and changes an innovation has on society, social transformations, acceptance, or rejection of the innovation, as well as modifications will be important issues. Changes in the social structures after the adoption of technology are related to cultural transmissions. The relationship between the innovation and the specific societies must first be understood empirically: the physical and abstract structure of the society must be clarified both before the arrival of the innovation and after its acceptance (Gillis 1999).

The arrival of metallurgy in most cases profoundly altering the fabric of the society. In the Aegean there is a great change during the course of the 3rd millennium from small villages just starting to use metal to cities, or archaic states with palace economies such as Knossos on Crete, Phylakopi on the island of Melos, and Lerna on the mainland.

During this time, the Aegean becomes a part of the extensive, long-distance Eastern Mediterranean trade sphere incorporating Egypt, Anatolia, the Levant coast and Mesopotamia. Although this trade system concerns mainly luxury items like ivory (Syria), spices (India), timber (Lebanon), textiles and perfume (Greece), silk (China), lapis lazuli (Afghanistan), etc., it also includes tin, a metal vital for the production of good-quality bronze. This need for tin, as well as for the status symbols necessary for the rising elite to establish and maintain their positions, led to great changes in the Aegean society during the course of the so-called Early Bronze Age (Gillis op.cit.; Nowicki 2000).

The origin of the dividing-line between the European and Asiatic zones of influence in the East Mediterranean is a very complex and still poorly researched subject. The present painful conflict between Greece and Turkey in the Aegean and on Cyprus is but the most recent continuation of the clash between two different regions, the beginning of which can be traced back to the Bronze Age. The differences stimulated progress and enriched the parts on both sides of this line. Although a great number of migrations and/or invasions led often to dramatic changes and moved the border line between Europe and Asia either to the West or to the East, it seems that exchange of ideas and goods, and cooperation played a much more important role in shaping the cultures, traditions, identities, customs and everyday life of the people living in that region. To sort out the role of conflicts, on one hand, and peaceful influence in the history of settlements in Crete, on the other, is the main task of one part of this project.

It may help to rethink the relationship between geography and history of the region, and to realize how much history is "written" by geography (Nowicki 2000).

Conclusions

There is no reason to separate the two, previously different, scientific traditions in archaeology: "classical" or Mediterranean and "prehistoric". By equalizing differences between these two research fields and between "Oriental" and "West", the positive role of the past and the potentials of these fields will be emphasized. The positive role of the past can be likewise illuminated through transnational scientific co-operations between European and non-European Eastern Mediterranean countries. The interactive co-operation with non-European countries, together with the large-scale perspectives, is one of the most important issues, and we suppose, one of the most important issues of this project.

Studies of the Central European material are essentially important, due to the fact that the area represents the geographic "bridge" between north and south, between east and west in the study of Mediterranean symbols in the South Scandinavian rock carvings tradition. The concept of symbols-interaction- social transformation can be seen as the connecting thought.

Only in the Eastern Mediterranean and Egypt can the **importance of written historical sources** be used fully as an aid in explaining cultural interactions and cultural diversities (Ben-Tor 1998). The combination of archaeological investigations and interpretations with the written sources, the global, large-scale perspectives, and the ethno-archaeological contemporary studies, creates an unique opportunity to emphasize the role of cultural identity and cultural interactionism in the past and in modern times, both in Europe and in surrounding areas.

We also expect to answer to one of the most important questions of the early history of Europe: how much the Eastern Mediterranean world, this key area between Europe and Asia, served as a possible transition point, which helped to adopt different elements of different cultures to make them acceptable by different social and political structures in different environments? How the cultural interactionism in the past influenced contemporary interactions? The unique combination of areas and aspects will create excellent opportunities to study both empirically and theoretically the mechanisms of cultural interaction and the acceptance, modification and/or rejection of innovation.

With the theoretical evolution of archaeology as a science of objects to one of cultural and social history, cultural interactionism seems to be more and more important as a tool in interpreting the past. Cultural interactionism in the Mediterranean World and in Temperate Europe is expressed by prehistoric material culture, changes in the use of landscape, settlement patterns and urbanization. The relevance of these important events in the past are of vital significance to contemporary societies, because past issues (urbanization, use of landscape, minorities, cultural diversities, and the preservations of cultural heritage) are no different in many cases than modern-day ones. An empirical and theoretical understanding of the mechanisms used on dealing with these issues as well as the spread of innovations and change resulting in part from such an understanding, will aid in understanding the present.

References

Bernal, Michael 1987. *Black Athena: The Afroasiatic Roots of Classical Civilization*, vol. 1. New Brunswick.

Ben-Tor, Amnon 1998. The fall of Canaanite Hazor – the "who" and "when" questions. In *Mediterranean Peoples in Transition*: 456-467. Jerusalem.

Gillis, Carole 1999. The Economic Value and Colour Symbolism of Tin. In Young, S., Pollard, M., Budd, P. & Ixer, R. (Eds.) *Metals in Antiquity*.

Gillis, Carole 2000 *in press*. Models of Social Structure and Economic Control. *Journées Ègéennes 1999. Les Modalités du Controle économique dans le monde Minoen et dans le monde Mycénien*. Ktema.

Kostakis, Kosta 1998. The past is ours. Images of Greek Macedonia. In Lynn Meskell (ed.) *Archaeology under Fire*. London & New York.

Larsson, Thomas 1997. Materiell kultur och religiösa symboler. *Arkeologiska studier vid Umeå universitet* 4. Umeå.

Larsson, Thomas 1999. The transmission of an elité ideology – Europe and the Near East in the second millennium BC. In Goldhahn, J. (ed.) *Rock Art as a Social Representation*. BAR International Series 794. Oxford.

Lewartowski, Kazimierz 1995. Myceanaean Social Structure: a view from simple graves. *Aegaeum* 12.

Mediterranean Peoples in Transition. 1998. Editors: S. Gitin, A. Mazar & E. Stern. Jerusalem.

Nowicki Krzysztof. 2000. *Defensible Sites in Crete, c. 1200-800 BC (LM IIIB/C through Early Geometric)*. Liege-Austin.

Olsson, Li 1999. Mediterranean Symbols in Late Bronze Age Rock Art on Southern Scandinavia. In Cruz, A.R. & Oosterbeek, Luiz. Curso de Atre Pre-Historica Europeia, Tomar.

Sherratt, Andrew 1993. What would a bronze-Age world system look like? Relations between Temperate Europe and the Mediterranean in later prehistory. *Journal of European Archaeology*, vol 1.2. Avebury.

Silberman, Neil Asher. 1998. Whose game is it anyway? The political and social transformations of American Biblical Archaeology. In Lynn Meskell (ed.) *Archaeology under Fire*. London & New York.

Werbart, Bozena 1996. Khazars or "Saltovo-Majaki Culture"? Prejudices about Archaeology and Ethnicity. *Current Swedish Archaeology* vol. 4. Stockholm.

Werbart, Bozena 1997. All these fantastic cultures? Concepts of archaeological cultures, identity and ethnicity. *Archaeologia Polona* vol 34:1966 Special Theme: Concepts of Archaeological Cultures. Warsaw-Lund.

Werbart, Bozena 2000. Review of Lynn Meskell (ed.). Archaeology under Fire. Nationalism, politics and heritage in the Eastern Mediterranean and Middle East. *NAR. Norwegian Archaeological Review*. Oslo.

Werbart, Bozena 2000 (in print). *Cultural Identity and Archaeology - a manifold theoretical perspective*. Arkeologiska Studier vid Umeå Universitet. Umeå.

Cultural Interactions in Europe and the Eastern Mediterranean during the Bronze Age (3000-500 BC)

Hazor – the Rise and Fall of the "Head of all Those Kingdoms"

Amnon Ben-Tor

The hill in upper Galilee, later to be known as the city of Hazor, was first settled in the first half of the third millennium B.C.E. The extent of the settlement is not yet known since the excavations penetrated to the appropriate depth only in a limited area. However, already in this early period, Hazor, located in southern Canaan (Israel of today), clearly maintained relations and shared a cultural affinity with northern Canaan (Syria and Lebanon of today). This is to be explained by the geographic proximity and by Hazor's location on the main north-south route connecting the two regions via the Lebanese Beq'a valley.

This shared cultural unity is manifest by two distinct characteristics of Hazor's Early Bronze Age material culture: first is the impressive amount of black and red polished pottery ('*Khirbet – Kerak - Ware*'), which forms an integral part of the ceramic assemblage retrieved at Hazor (Greenberg 1997:17-24). Second are the cylinder seal impressions with geometric motifs placed as decorative designs (?) on the shoulders of storage-jars: these share a great similarity with cylinder seals found in Syria and even beyond, as far west as – for example – the site of *Lerna* in Greece (Ben-Tor 1978: 63-69; 1985:14-19).

In spite of the collapse of the Early Bronze Age political system in Canaan which took place in the 24th-23rd centuries B.C.E., Hazor's 'Syrian connection' was maintained also during the next period, the Intermediate Bronze Age. This is clearly shown by the ceramic assemblage uncovered at the site, which is identical (some of it may indeed have been imported) with that characterizing such Syrian sites as *Tell Mardikh (Ebla)* IIB 1-2 and *Hama* J (Ben-Tor 1998: 275).

A major change in the history of Hazor took place in the first quarter of the second millennium B.C.E., during the Middle Bronze Age. Sometime in the second half of the 18th century B.C.E, Hazor becomes a major city. It was no longer confined to the southern hill, measuring some 10-15 acres (the 'acropolis') where the settlement started: it now 'spills over' and spreads over a large area ('the lower city') to the north of the acropolis. Hazor becomes a metropolis covering some 200 acres with an estimated population of 20-30,000 people. The city was surrounded by massive fortifications typical of the time, similar to those known from various other sites all over Canaan. These included an enormous earth-embankment protected by a moat, city walls, and several 'Syrian'-gates. At least three temples were erected in different parts of the city (Yadin 1972: 50-66, 75-79, 96-98; Ben-Tor 2000: 248).

Significantly – this is also the first time that Hazor appears in the historical record: it is mentioned in the Egyptian Execration Texts of the so-called Posner group, dated to the time of the XIII Egyptian dynasty (Posner 1940: 73:E 15; Yadin 1972:1-2). The inclusion of Hazor in those Execration Texts indicates that it was considered to be important enough in the 18th century, to 'merit' this kind of "voodoo-like" practice.

Fragments of eight statues of Egyptian rulers give another indication of Hazor's 'Egyptian connection' during the Middle Bronze Age. Unfortunately all but one of the Egyptian kings (or dignitaries) represented in these statues cannot be identified. The one exception is a small sphinx inscribed with the name of the twelfth Egyptian dynasty monarch *Amenemhat* III. All the other statue fragments – all of very high quality, are most probably also to be dated to the same period, judging by their style. In our judgment all these statues pre-date by several decades the foundation, or at least the rise to significance, of the city of Hazor. They thus seem to have arrived at Hazor not directly from Egypt, during the life time of the rulers in question, but perhaps via Syria, and if so – most probably from *Byblos*. Interestingly – several of these statues were found in the destruction layer of the Late Bronze Age palace, in a context several centuries later than the time of manufacture of the statues. They were apparently kept in the palace as heirlooms and exhibited there as objects of prestige.

In the second half of the 18th century B.C.E. the city of Hazor plays a distinctive role in more than a dozen tablets uncovered in the royal palace of *Mari* on the Euphrates. Hazor is the <u>only</u> site in southern Canaan included in this correspondence, testifying, again, to its importance. Mari's influential king, *Zimri-Lim* may have had family relations by marriage, with the ruling family at Hazor. From the documents one can learn about the important economic and political role played by Hazor at the time (Bonechi, 1992): it probably ruled over a large area covering the entire *Hula* valley, extending to the *Bashan* in the east and as far north as the southern *Beq'a*. Caravans carrying a variety of precious goods travelled between Hazor via Syria and *Mari* – to *Babylon*. Several documents, similar to the Mari ones, found their way (as heirlooms?) to the somewhat later palace of Late Bronze Age Hazor. One such document mentions enormous amounts of goods (such as 500 garments, 3000 silver and 1000 gold rivets, 2000 bows and much more) that were to be sent from Hazor to Mari, clearly testifying to Hazor's wealth Horowitz and Wasserman 2000:169-174).

For several years now, we are uncovering the palace of Hazor's ruling family during the Late Bronze Age, appropriately located in the center of the city's acropolis. This palace was constructed in the 16th century B.C.E., and is thus somewhat later than the one contemporary with the Mari period.

The palace is a magnificent structure as befits the ruling family of such a wealthy and important city. It measures close to 2000 sq.m., it's walls are about 3 meters thick, built of mud-brick on a massive stone foundation and lined with orthostats of high quality. The plan and architectural details of the palace show an extremely close affinity with the contemporary palace uncovered in the city of *Alalakh*, indicating a degree of architectural *koine* in the mid-second millennium B.C.E. in the region (Ben-Tor 1999:22-39). This northern 'flavor' of Hazor's material culture is further indicated by the nature of the finds originating from the palace, and the *objets d'art* in particular: Lion orthostats, cylinder seals, jewelry, figurines – all bear close resemblance to north Canaanite counterparts, uncovered in such sites as *Kamid el-Loz, Ugarit* and *Alalakh*.

The ceramic assemblage unearthed in the Late Bronze Age contexts of Hazor, is a clear reflection of its close, as well as far reaching foreign contacts. The majority of the ceramic repertoire constitutes of the typical local Canaanite types, but together with them, Cypriote, Mycenean, Hittite, North Syrian and Egyptian vessels, and local imitations of such vessels are found.

While Late Bronze Age Hazor continues to be an integral part of the Canaanite cultural sphere, politically it is, like the rest of Canaan, under direct Egyptian rule. This is clearly indicated by its mention in several lists of towns conquered by pharaohs of the New Kingdom such as *Thutmosis* III, *Amenophis* II and *Seti* II (*Pritchard* 1955:242ff). Most interesting are two letters sent by *Abdi-Tirshi* king of Hazor to the Egyptian pharaoh *Amenophis* IV, found at *el-Amarna (Yadin* 1972: 7-9). In these letters the king of Hazor is referred to by himself and by others (the king of Tyre) by the title 'king', a title unparalleled in all other cases of mention or rulers of Canaanite cities in the *Amarna* archive, clearly reflecting the importance of Hazor.

Whether or not Hazor is mentioned in an Egyptian inscription dated to the reign of *Ramesses* II in the first half of the 13th century B.C.E. (Yadin 1972 : 7) – is still undecided. It is thus not certain, at this stage of our research, whether the story of Late Bronze Age Hazor comes to an end with *Seti* II, that is at the end of the 13th century B.C.E., or in the days of *Rameses* II, a few decades later. However – when the end came – it was sudden and violent: the entire city was destroyed in a huge conflagration. The palace is covered by a layer of more than half a meter of burnt timber, ashes and collapsed and, at times, melted mud-brick, indicating that the fire reached a temperature of over 1200 degrees centigrade.

So thorough was the destruction, that its memory was kept alive for centuries. It is described thus in the book of Joshua:

> "And Joshua turned back at that time, and took Hazor, and smote its king with the sword; For Hazor formerly was the head of all those kingdoms…and he burned Hazor with fire…but none of the cities that stood on mounds did Israel burn except Hazor only; that Joshua burned" (Joshua 11:10-13).

Who was indeed responsible for that destruction is still a matter of controversy. However – with the disappearance of Hazor, 'head of those kingdoms' the arena was free and the country was wide open to be settled by those – among whom were most probably also the Israelites who "took all that land, the hill country and all the *Negeb* and all the land of *Goshen*, and the lowland and the *Arabah*, and the hill country of Israel and its lowland, from Mount *Halak* that rises toward *Se'ir*, as far as *Ba'al–gad* in the valley of Lebanon, below *Mount Hermon*" (Joshua 11:16-17).

Bibliography

Ben-Tor, A., 1978 *Cylinder Seals of Third Millennium Palestine,* Bulleyin of the American Schools of Oriental Research Supplement Series, no. 22, Cambridge Mass.
  1985 The Glyptic Art of Early Bronze Age Palestine and its Foreign Relations, pp. 14-19, in E. Lipinski (ed) – *The Land of Israel Cross-Roads of Civilizations*, Uitgeverij Peters, Leuven.
  1988 Tel-Hazor 1998, Notes and News, *Israel Exploration Journal* 48:275
  1999 Excavating Hazor: Did the Israelites Destroy the Canaanite City? *Biblical Archaeology Review,* 25 (3) 1999: 22-39.
  2000 Tel-Hazor 2000, Notes and News, *Israel Exploration Journal* 50 (3-4): 243-249
Bonechi, M., Relationes Amicales Syro-Palestiniennes: Mari et Hazor Au XVIIe Siecle A.J.C. in: Durand, J-M (ed.) *Memoires de N.A.B.U. Florilegium Marianum. Recueil d'etudes en l'honneur de Michel Fleury*, Paris, pp.9-22
Greenberg, R., in Ben-Tor at al. (eds.) *Hazor V,* The Israel Exploration Society, The Hebrew University, Jerusalem.
Horowitz, W., and Wasserman, N., An Old Babylonian Letter from Hazor with Mention of Mari and Ekallātum, *Israel Exploration Journal* 50 (3-4): 169-174.
Posner, G., *Princes et Pays d'Asie et de Nubie. Textes hiératique sur des figurines d'envoûtement du Moyen Empire,* Bruxelles.
Pritchard, J.B., *Ancient Near Eastern Texts Relating to the Old Testament,* Princeton, New Jersey, Princeton University Press.
Yadin, Y., *Hazor: The head of all those Kingdoms (Joshua 11:10)* The schweich Lecture Series of the British Academy 1970, London, Oxford University Press.

Cultural Encounters
Symbols from the Mediterranean World in the South Scandinavian Rock Carving Tradition during the Bronze Age

Li Winter

Abstract

The aim of this article is to present a number of symbols and symbolic structures in the South Scandinavian rock carving tradition and material culture during the Bronze Age, which show similarities with features of religious practices and belief systems in the Mediterranean cultures from the same period.

The symbols presented in this article are *the ship, the bull, the double-axe, the warrior and the chariot, male- and female figurines*. The use of the particular symbols seems to be concentrated in the province of Bohuslän on the western coast of Sweden, and to a certain extent in Denmark. A few examples of this feature are also found in other parts of Southern Sweden, mainly in the provinces considered central areas during the Bronze Age (Scania and Östergötland).

The various reasons for interaction and transmission of symbols and ideas between Scandinavia, Europe and the Mediterranean during the Early and Late Bronze Age are considered, and discussed in terms of a theoretical and methodological strategy for the interpretation of exchange and cultural interaction in a Bronze Age context. The spread of knowledge of the meaning of foreign symbols could possibly be closely connected with items of status and prestige, shown in the archaeological record, and closely linked to the rise of chiefly Elites on the Continent.

Introduction

This article is based on the thesis that I am working on, and the aim is to present symbols from the Mediterranean area in the rock carving tradition and the material culture in Southern Scandinavia during the Bronze Age, 1800-500 BC. The main lines of inquiry concern the transmission of symbols, ideas and conceptions through Bronze Age Europe, and how different ritual practices and believes were introduced and adopted in many parts of Europe through various forms of human interaction and exchange systems. The material consists of symbols such as ships, bulls and acrobats, horned helmets, human figures, animals, as well as certain objects, decorations, house constructions that are represented as rock carvings in the province of Bohuslän on the West Coast of Sweden, and as mobile art in Denmark. My studies of the south Scandinavian rock carving tradition show so far that the use of symbols that can be related to the eastern Mediterranean are found mainly in this particular regions, with a few exceptions in the central areas of the South Scandinavian Bronze Age. This pattern could indicate that the knowledge of foreign traditions linked the higher strata in the society together, and also created the intermediate link with the development of chiefly elites on the Continent.

The Bronze Age period in Europe can be seen as a historical phase when many societies in Temperate and Mediterranean Europe transformed into socially differentiated or stratified systems. This social change was most certainly linked to the development of new forms of leadership, which required (or stimulated the development of) a different cosmology/belief system, in which leadership and divinity in some cases were brought into conjunction (Larsson 1999:49).

Throughout the prehistory of Europe a relatively extensive transmission of symbols and material culture took place. Did new religious beliefs and mentalities follow the transmission over large areas? And did the original function and meaning of the symbols change in a different social context? Studies of the central European material are essentially important, due to the fact that the area represents the geographical 'bridge' between areas separated both culturally and geographically (Kristiansen & Larsson *in prep*).

The material and theories presented here are based on a large amount of archaeological data, and are not presented in detail in this article. I will show only very brief examples of how some of the symbols were depicted and used in different areas. I will also briefly discuss the need of a theoretical strategy for the interpretation of cultural exchange and cultural interaction in Bronze Age Europe.

Previous research

It is not a widely accepted fact in the Swedish research tradition, that the South Scandinavian cosmology depicted in the rock carving tradition and material culture to a certain extent were influenced by ideas originating in the Mediterranean cultures. Because of this, studies of human interaction and symbolic-religious transmission in Bronze Age Europe has been somewhat neglected. Rock carvings were seen as images of local events and religious rituals that were created regionally without impact from other areas and cultures.

For archaeologists active in the late 19th century the transmission was something obvious, although they worked from the concept of diffusion. The history of research of this interaction and exchange is indeed worth going back to, although with a slightly different approach, due to the constantly increasing knowledge of archaeological material culture in different areas. It should most certainly be a help in the process of developing a 'new' strategy for explaining cultural contacts and change in a Bronze Age context, and serve to illuminate the mechanisms that brought this change to happen.

The fact that there are certain symbols and also objects with parallels in the eastern Mediterranean cultures, strongly indicate that there were connections and trading networks in Europe and the Mediterranean during the Bronze Age. I believe that it is and important and it could prove to be fruitful to try to illuminate the interaction between different areas in both local and broader geographical perspective, as well as the mechanisms involved in the process of cultural change cultural contacts.

Rock carvings and dating

Very few of the rock carvings have been dated absolutely. In a few cases relative dating can be achieved, based on comparisons with representations of identifiable objects in the engravings and similar motifs on bronze objects. A relative chronology based on the stylistic features of ship representations have been worked out by Mats P. Malmer; Bertil Almgren also worked on the dating problem (Malmer 1981; Almgren 1987). Dating by means of studying definable superpositions and the identification of datable objects are another possible way of establishing an inner chronology for the South Scandinavian rock carving tradition (e.g. Burenhult 1980).

To make this very simple, rock carving ships without a lot of ornamental details date to the Early Bronze Age, and consequently, those with elaborate decorative details are dated to Late Bronze Age. Rich figurative scenes are thought to be of Late Bronze Age date, with a few exceptions of course. The bronze objects and figurines are dated according to the six-period system worked out for Scandinavian Bronze Age by Oscar Montelius. Acta Archaeologica vol. 67-1996 provides a recent compilation of articles on absolute and relative chronology in Bronze Age Europe (Randsborg (ed.) 1996). Kristian Kristiansen has also compiled a broader work on the Bronze Age in Scandinavia and Europe, where the different chronologies are correlated (Kristiansen 1998) and John Collis did the same on the European Iron Age (Collis 1989)

The South Scandinavian rock carvings

Rock carvings are found all over Scandinavia, with the principal centre in western Sweden, in the province of Bohuslän. The rich figurative scenes are exceptional and the Tanum area are on the World Heritage list provided by UNESCO (Bengtsson & Hygen 1999).

Most of the rock art localities are found in the area between the Bronze Age shoreline and the arable land. My study concentrated on the province of Bohuslän, due to the enormous amount of rock carving figures and also to the variation of figures among the material. Other major engraving areas in Sweden and neighbouring countries are considered where the material is of relevance for the study (Fig. 1). In the province of Bohuslän there are a few major engraving areas, with smaller (less than 200 figures) localities distributed in the landscape (Bertilsson 1987). These can be seen as special places in the landscape, used for ritual and religious purposes, and the engraving localities were probably used continually over a long period of time (Fig. 2). Thomas B. Larsson has suggested that the spatial picture could perhaps be compared to the religious organisation in the Aegean and the Near East with its wide distribution of shrines used by the rural population and a few more elaborate structures such as the palaces/temples devoted to priestly and royal religion. The structuring picture of social and ritual space could have been fairly similar, and it is an inspiring analogy, but it is important to stress that the features indicating royal/chiefly religion and folk religion are very different when comparing Scandinavia and the Eastern Mediterranean (Larsson 1999:57f).

In the following, I will only briefly show a few examples of the symbols and combinations of symbols in the South Scandinavian and in the East Mediterranean world. For a more thorough presentation of the similarities I refer to Larsson 1997; 1999; Olsson 1996; 1997; 1998, 1999, 2000.

Symbols and meaning

The Bronze Age rock carvings may represent both ideology as well as religion, there is no opposition between these two concepts. Religion is a part of the ideology, and the ideology is depending on religious practices and rituals for its maintenance.

For the people of the Bronze Age the meaning and function of the rock art symbols was a natural part of life. Symbols gain meaning from their contexts and contextualized meanings are of many kinds. Myths, dances and other types of performance are the primary contexts of symbolic meaning, and this is only rarely available to the archaeologists. The myths and narratives associated with religion can be materialised in paintings, decorations, consumption goods, ritual structures etc, which are often bound together by common rituals. In the past, such different material remains would have been understood as being part of common ritual events and myths, while in archaeology they are separated and defined as different contexts, labelled burials, standing stones votive offerings, sanctuaries and rock art (Kristiansen 1999b: 537f).

Many of the elements of religion such as processions and dances, garlands and masks, sacraments and rituals, may not leave behind the slightest remaining trace (Burkert 1985:10). Occasionally early pictorial art may help, and by analysing the depictions in the rock carving tradition the single representations can be an instrument for the interpretation and understanding of transmission of foreign ideas. If it is possible to distinguish certain local/autonomous traces, elements or combinations in the rock carvings, foreign ideas and symbols may be separated from the local tradition/religion. And as Kristian Kristiansen has pointed out, by studying symbols in their different contexts in a broader geographical perspective, it could be possible to try to detect recurring and meaningful structures in the archaeological record (Kristiansen 1999b: 538). The concept of the warrior can be used as an illuminating example, and was probably a widely spread phenomenon, shown by the distribution of parade arms in Europe during the Late Bronze Age/early Iron Age (Mohen 1985:58f) (Fig. 3).

Many motives occur time after time in different cultures all over the world, and it is off course important to be aware that the symbols do not always have the same meaning. Symbols often change character over time, as well as meaning (Bengtsson & Hygen 1999:14). These kinds of changes are important to consider when parallels between different areas and cultures are made. Rock carvings were created during a long period of time, and traditions and motifs could have been in use for several generations. Religious beliefs and religious symbolism are often quite conservative, and similar depictions could be part of a more or less widespread network of a cosmological symbolic system. The meaning and use of symbols developed in a cultural framework, but culture is never completely isolated or completely open and receptive.

Both in prehistoric and modern societies culture is formed and changed through meetings between the well known and the unknown. This is true for technology, ideas and also for symbolic value and meanings (Bengtsson & Hygen 1999:88).

The archaeological interpretations of South Scandinavian rock carvings and other forms of Bronze Age material culture would certainly benefit a great deal if a broader geographical perspective was used in "a relevant context". As Thomas B. Larsson pointed out, we have to move away from simplistic diffusionism and question the theory of "local autonomous development". Instead it is analyses of the social strategies behind the transmission of a certain type of artefacts over vast areas that must be taken into consideration (Larsson 1999:60). The problem is to find a general methodology for analysing contact between prehistoric societies and the cultural changes associated with that contact, and at the same time consider the complexity of exchange relations. During the Bronze Age a by all means international trading network developed, based on the spread of metallurgy and exchange of objects of prestige. This made the different regions dependent on each other, despite differences in the cultural traditions. The relationship between external vs. internal factors in the complex process of change is indeed a central question, and there is a need for theoretical framework in the interpretation and explication of how cultural contact and cultural change work. One example are discussions of centre/periphery relations and "a world system approach" (Kristiansen 1987; 1998; 1999a; 1999b: 333-343).

The ship

The most frequently occurring symbol in the South Scandinavian rock carving tradition is the figure of a ship. Among the thousands of ship engravings, there are a number which show striking similarities with engraved and painted ship-figures from the eastern Mediterranean area.

The ship representations show similarities in both the construction of the outline and in decorative details. In some cases the Scandinavian representations occur in settings which remind of both Egyptian and Greek religious beliefs, like the Egyptian grave-paintings and relief images, where votive ships are being offered to the deceased or to the God (Burenhult 1973:159; 1979:17). One can find examples from the Minoan and the Mycenean contexts as well. In the Scandinavian rock carving tradition, there are several examples where a miniature ship is being carried by human figures and depictions of votive-offerings are found in the province of Bohuslän on the west coast of Sweden, with a few examples in the provinces of Uppland and Östergötland on the east coast. (Fig. 4a-e). Here, relevant questions concern coincidence and autonomous development.

In the pictorial world of Swedish rock carvings, there are numbers of ship engravings, which show typological similarities with ship representations from the Mediterranean area. The similarities especially concern the construction of the hull, the stern decoration, the occurrences of mast and/or sail, the presence of a ram, a possible cabin, and the decorative details on the gunwale. An important observation is that most of the Scandinavian rock carving ships do not show any similarities with the Mediterranean material; perhaps some of the rock carving ships show constructions such as outriggers, a very reasonable explanation concerning the way the ships are depicted. They can be compared with the Egyptian way of depicting things and people from the side, with the hidden parts shown in profile so that the representation would be complete (Österholm 1996:4).

In Gisslegärde, Tossene parish in the province of Bohuslän on the West Coast of Sweden, there is a group of rock carving ships with very unusual hull constructions. To my knowledge, there is no other ship engraving of this kind in Sweden at present. This type of ship has a contour carved hull, with a massive extension of the keel, a depiction of a ram, and the stern is extended and turned upwards. This group of Swedish rock carving ships show similarities with depictions of the Greek war galleys, painted on vases from the Geometric period, about 700 BC. During the early first millenium BC an important discovery was made, a nautical technical revolution which made the Greeks masters of the sea. It was the ram, a massive projection at the bow of the ship, constructed to tear the hull of the enemy's ships into pieces. The earliest representation of a ship with a ram was found on a bronze fibula from Athens, dated to about 850 B.C. Depictions of galleys without ram appear around 1150 BC, and the introduction of the ram is thought to have taken place during the intervening centuries (Casson 1994:51). An interesting observation is that the Swedish rock carving ships with the ram-detail are depicted together with symbols like chariots, horses, human figures with weapons and processions, a structure similar to the combinations of motifs on the Dipylonvases. The vases were used as grave markers, for the society's elite only, and the motifs are thought to represent scenes from the burial ritual (Castleden 1991:37-51) (Fig. 5 a).

Strange types of rock carving ships are those furnished with a cabin. They were only found in Bohuslän, and this kind is totally absent in the Mediterranean, although there were ships with cabins. The ship to the left is from the province of Bohuslän, with two cabins on the gunwale, and a single vertical line in the hull. The ship to the right is a drawing of a ship engraved on a mobile block of stone from Hyria in Boetia in Greece. The shape of the hull and the cabins are almost identical with the ship from Bohuslän, apart from a few lines in the hull, and that there are two vertical lines leaping downwards from the gunwale. If we recall the inscription in Hagia Sofia in Istanbul, where a Swedish Viking actually made a runic inscription with a meaning similar to "Kilroy was here", one could end up with the idea of a Nordic Bronze Age man sketching an image of a ship on a piece of stone when out on a trading expedition (Fig. 5b).

Some of the scenes involving the ship symbol in Scandinavia could depict a myth or a story originating in the Mediterranean area. The composition and meaning of the scene may be similar, but shaped to fit with different societies (Fig. 5c).

The sun symbol or the circle figure

In Egypt the ships were sometimes used as the vessels transporting the sun god. At daytime the god sailed over the sky in the morning boat, and at nightfall he entered the underworld in his evening boat. The dead were transported to the other side in the night boat, and in the picture the dead are asking for permission to enter the boat for the journey to afterlife. Among the south Scandinavian rock carvings there are several symbols representing the sun, called sun-disks, depicted in combination with ships, by itself or carried on a stand. Scholars believed that this was a sign of a 'sun-cult', religious manifestations in honour of a sun god, where the god travelled over the sky in a ship or in a wagon. This idea should have diffused through much of Europe from the Near East, Egypt and Mycenean Greece. Examples of South Scandinavian "sun ships", were found in the regions of Östergötland the on the eastern coast of Sweden and also in Bohuslän. The precise meaning of the symbol is difficult to decide, but this indicates that South Scandinavia shared parts of a widely spread cosmological symbolism. Probably the most famous Scandinavian example of a symbolic representation of the widely spread myth of the sun-chariot in its travel over the sky, is the find from Trundholm in Denmark, dated to around 1350 BC (Larsson 1996) (Fig. 6).

Ships with a sail

The question of whether the Scandinavian rock carving ships were depicted with sails or not, has been raised many times, as well as whether the art of sailing was known at all in Scandinavia during the Bronze Age. Some scholars claim that the art of sailing first became known during the 6th-7th century AD. This notion is based on the fact that the oldest, and only find of a Scandinavian ship furnished with sail is from the 6th century AD. An interesting observation is that there are representations of rock carving ships with details that cannot be interpreted as anything else than a mast, strays and sail, and which show typological similarities with ship representations from the Mediterranean area (e.g. Burenhult 1973). There is a complete correspondence in the way of depicting the details showing mast and strays (Fig 5d).

Acrobats, bulls and snake goddesses

The ship symbol is not the only symbol with parallels in the Mediterranean world. A number of other figures and objects support the theory of influences from the Mediterranean cultures. One of the most outstanding depictions is the acrobat, found as rock carving only in the province of Bohuslän and Dalsland, and as bronze miniatures in Denmark. Some scholars are of the opinion that acrobatic games in honour of the gods originated in the Near East, and spread over the Mediterranean world during the Bronze Age. Representations of acrobats are known in Syria since around 1700 BC, and are present in Crete since 1600 BC. Acrobatic games were also popular in Egypt, and there are several wall paintings and reliefs showing this motif, often as a sequence of movements, like a cartoon.

In Minoan Crete, bull leaping was a major ingredient in the religious practices and took place in the palaces and portrayals of bull-leaping scenes seem to be especially common in the palace of Knossos. Only a skilled person, trained especially for this purpose could have performed the difficult leaps and somersaults. The acrobats are often beautifully dressed, with jewellery and elaborate hairdo, and it has been suggested that the leapers were of noble origin (Castleden 1991). Dickinson has pointed out, that elaborate hairdo was seen as a social marker and that it had an important ritual meaning in the Minoan culture, and the lavish hairstyles were for the elite only (Dickinson 1994: 89f; 278; 282; 302).

The Minoan acrobats seem to be of both sexes, but this is not clearly marked in the Scandinavian material. An interesting observation is that depiction of acrobats and ships seems to be a Scandinavian phenomenon. There are no pictures of this combination in the Mediterranean material. An interesting parallel to this feature in ancient literary sources, is where acrobats are said to perform on boat models placed on land in honour of the ageing God of Vegetation, a cult reaching back to the Minoan period (Almgren 1927:81ff) (Fig. 7a-n).

The miniature bronze figurines from Grevensvænge in Denmark, from the late Scandinavian Bronze Age, share certain features with rituals and religious symbols from the Mediterranean cultures. The find originally consisted of two horned men with axes, one standing female figure with a long skirt and an outstretched hand, and three acrobats bent backwards, dressed in short cord-like skirts. The figures were all set upon perforated pegs, as if for mounting on some organic material. A reconstruction of the find has been made after comparison with rock carving scenes and engravings made on bronze razors (Burenhult 2000:115ff) (Fig. 8a).

The cult of the bull was of central importance in the Minoan and Mycenean belief system, and depictions of bulls in different settings are a common feature. Many of the Scandinavian bull engravings are shown together with axes, men with axes, acrobats holding axes while hanging on the bull's horns. The axe is a common feature in ritual deposits throughout Bronze Age Europe, and the existence of certain symbolic codes, common to the Bronze Age people, is not unlikely. The bronze metallurgy certainly played a major part in the distribution, and the knowledge certainly spread through varying forms of human/social interaction and exchange.

Other important symbols and figures in the Minoan and Mycenean cultures were fish- and bird motifs, stags, double-axes, fabulous beasts, and miniature female statuettes called 'Snake Goddesses', because they are often shown together with snakes. Such figures and symbols were represented in the Fårdal find from Denmark, dated to the Middle Bronze Age (Fig. 8b).

The Fårdal group consisted of two stag figures, a double representation of the same animal with a little duck in the middle, a snake and a kneeling female figure, dressed in a loin-cloth similar to that worn by the acrobat in the Grevensvænge find. The female figure of the Fårdal find is holding one hand over her breast and lifting the other upwards. The snake has a loop on the neck, and it has been suggested that the female originally held the snake on a lead (Glob 1969; Burenhult 2000:115ff). The Fårdal goddess has its counterparts in the snake goddesses of Crete. Like the Fårdal goddess, these are also dressed in skirts, have bare breasts, wear headgear and are holding snakes. A large number of snake goddesses have been found in the Mediterranean world, and there are also other goddesses together with different kinds of animals (Burkert 1985; Castleden 1991; Higgins 1992) (Fig. 9).

A European weight system?

During the late Bronze Age, about 700-500 BC, another type of small female bronze figurines occur in the votive deposits, together with finds of a more 'female' character, like earrings, combs and belt-bags. The female figurines are wearing a single or a double necklace, and are usually called 'the goddess with the necklace'. These goddesses are bare breasted, they are holding their hands over the stomach, the arms forming a loop.

A rock carving showing this goddess has been found on the island of Tjörn, on the west coast of Sweden, linking the rock carving tradition to the material culture (Pettersson & Kristiansson 1977:41). There are examples of 'the goddess with the necklace' in many parts of Europe, for example in Sweden, Denmark and Germany; they are all very alike, about ten centimetres high, and with a uniform weight of about 107 gram. The female figurines have been seen as a part of a widespread weight system, providing a link in the trading and exchange systems between Scandinavia, Europe and the Mediterranean (Malmer 1992:377-388). Similar figurines were found in the Mediterranean area, and are connected with religious practices such as dedications to the gods. These figurines most likely had both a religious and a more commercial meaning: one meaning does not exclude the other (Malmer 1999:33-41).

There are also male bronze figurines in Scandinavia which have their counterparts in the Mediterranean area, such as the hoard find from Stockhult in Scania, dated to the Early Bronze Age. The find consisted of both male and female objects such as socked axes, golden neck collars and belt-boxes, and two male bronze figurines. The Stockhult figures have clearly marked eyebrow bows and big noses, they were wearing conical hats and 'shorts' (Burenhult 1999:416f). These figures are almost identical with a number of male bronze figurines from Crete, and they are also represented in different parts of Europe. Many of these Cretan figures are wearing the same conical hats, have marked eyebrow bows and big noses, and similar shorts. This kind of male figures with horns or hats, are connected to conceptions of rulers/kings/divinities, and in the South Scandinavian case the male figurines from the Stockhult find as well as the ones from Grevensvænge, add significance to the institution of twin rulers in Scandinavia, an institution originating in the Mycenean concept of the wanax king but adapted to a different social environment (Kristiansen 1999b: 547ff). Other Minoan motifs are star patterns, meanders, geometric design, fish-and bird motifs and symbols interpreted as holy trees or double axes, or as a purely decorative detail, and are found on objects such as razors, knives of different kinds, tweezers, necklaces with oval end-plates, swords, a comb, two Celts and a spearhead made of bronze. Both rock carving ships and objects made of bronze in South Scandinavia are decorated with symbols originating in the Mediterranean area. From the Minoan Crete, the spiral ornamentation spread through Bronze Age Europe and finally reached Scandinavia. Ship figures on bronze objects have often been somewhat underestimated in archaeological literature, while the rock carving ships have been the main topic in several monographs. In combination, studies of ship figures on bronzes and on rock could most certainly produce fruitful results concerning iconographic interpretations, as well as providing relative dating for the combination of figures (e.g. Kaul 1995).

Cultural encounters - the journey to the far North

To return to some of the initial questions: We have seen that there are similarities in the material culture and in the use of certain symbols between the Mediterranean area and South Scandinavia. But why should the Bronze Age society in Scandinavia integrate a foreign belief system, with new rituals and symbolic codes? The process of cultural change and the effects of the rapid growth of emerging trading networks are indeed an important part of this study. One possible theoretical approach is to develop and explicate a general methodology for examining contact situations using archaeological data (e.g. Wells 1980; Kristiansen 1987; 1999a). In the following I will try to give an outline of possible reasons for interaction, and also the most likely trading routes.

Scandinavia was a part of a long-distance exchange system, with networks over East-, West-, Central- and South Europe, which is shown in finds of imports from both Early and Late Bronze Age. The rivers were important trading routes in Central Europe, and the commercial networks from the Mediterranean seems to have passed Massilia (Marseilles), along the river Rhône northwards, or by land from Northern Italy over the Alpine passes. It has been suggested that the trading routes at sea took place in stages, and went along the shores of the Mediterranean and Western Europe to the North (Stjernqvist 1962:85f). The contacts with Europe during the Bronze Age/Early iron Age follow two main directions: one link from Mycenae towards Southern Italy and the other route leading towards Central and Northern Europe. The first can be inferred by the finds of LH I (1550 BC) pottery in the Lipari Islands, and LH II (1500 BC) wares have been found in southern Italy and in Albania (Larsson 1999:55). It has been suggested that the Baltic amber was the repayment for various items of prestige originating in the Mediterranean. In fig. 3 the routes for amber trade are shown together with find-spots of bronze parade arms (such as helmets, breastplates, shields and greaves) dating from the end of the Bronze Age/beginning of the Iron Age (12th-7th centuries BC). These finds indicate that similar conceptions of warfare and probably also of the system of chiefs existed in this period. It is important to be aware that it is not only visible objects that could have been exchanged; knowledge about ideas, myths and belief and other forms of non-material communication, which are normally hidden from archaeologists, might be the missing prestige valuables coming from the East Mediterranean world (e.g. Larsson 1997; 1999; Olsson 1998; 1999).

Manifestations of an elite?

The rise of chiefly elites in Europe was most certainly connected to the rapid growth of long-distance trade systems during the Early Iron Age (Scandinavian Late Bronze Age). Objects manufactured in Greek and Etruscan workshops were identified in burial contexts in west-central Europe, and much has been written about trade between Mediterranean societies and central Europe. The main focus has often been the chronology of the trade, the probable origin of imported objects, and routes by which they were brought to central Europe. Some of the most significant finds have been made at Vix, the Heuneburg, Grafenbül and Eberdingen-Hochdorf. Very little effort has been made to understand the connections between the interactions that brought the imports to central Europe and the cultural changes which occurred in the regions in which the imports are most abundant (Wells 1980:ix). There are imports in Scandinavia, objects of prestige and in the end power. One example of long distance trading networks is the so-called Balkåkra drum from Scania in Sweden, dated to the Early South Scandinavian Bronze Age. It is interpreted as a cult object connected with sun worshipping (Fig. 10). This object has its counterpart in Hasfalva in Hungary, and the stylistic features reveal that they were manufactured in the same workshop (e.g. Burenhult 2000:418; Larsson 1996; 1997). Another example of imports from South Europe is the find of a hoard at Hassle in the region of Närke in Middle Sweden, dated to Late Bronze Age. The find consists of one bronze cauldron probably originating from some Greek colony, two buckets made of bronze of Italian origin, twelve bronze discs and two swords from the Hallstatt region (Burenhult 2000:100). The main issue in the future should be to examine the effects of commercial interactions on the societies involved (Wells 1980:ix).

The theories put forward in this article are based on a large amount of archaeological data, and a part of my thesis in progress. By attempting to formulate models for various mechanisms of exchange, interaction and processes of change based upon for example ethnographic and historical literature dealing with cultural connections, it may be possible to approach questions concerning the transmission of symbols and cosmology from the eastern Mediterranean cultures. It is not a question of simply borrowing models from ethnographic contexts and applying them to archaeological problems, since no contact situations are identical. But in this kind of processes, there are certain regularities in the patterns by which cultural changes occur. Working with these regularities, and developing general models for change, could be useful in the study of changes and cultural interaction during the South Scandinavian Bronze Age/Early European Iron Age (Wells 1980:x).

By making journeys to distant and unknown parts of the world, local chiefs in Northern and Central Europe could increase their prestige and authority through their knowledge and access to powerful foreign rituals and ideas

(Larsson 1999:55). From the mid 6th century BC Greek and Etruscan objects began to appear within the West Hallstatt Culture, and the imports were connected almost exclusively with wine drinking. In the Hallstatt zone, wine drinking was associated with elaborate burials and spectacular drinking vessels, imported for use by the elite. These vessels were not prestige goods destined for redistribution, but were goods reserved for use and burial within the highest stratum of the social scale. In the lower Rhône Basin, the situation was quite different, the finds consist mostly of simple drinking vessels. Imports were rare in graves and most of the Mediterranean imports were found as debris in settlement deposits. The custom of wine-drinking was seen as something rare and exotic in isolated areas, for use by the elite only as a symbol of power and status. The knowledge about new customs and traditions and the objects connected to these, provided the elite with something that was not available to every man. To gain this knowledge, it was necessary to travel, and it was during the journeys that objects and traditions spread through Europe (Dietler 1996).

In Bronze Age Europe and South Scandinavia the signs of social inequality are clearly visible in the archaeological record. In Denmark the distribution of metal objects (gold and bronze) in graves could be interpreted as an expression of social structure of a certain district. The distribution of metal artefacts is correlating to the quality of land in historic times, and could indicate the existence of chiefdom in Bronze Age Denmark (Randsborg 1974). The assumed rise of the institution of the warrior is correlating to the social development in Europe during the Late Bronze Age and Early Iron Age (Bertilsson 1999:750). The building of big burial monuments such as the Kivik cairn or the Sagaholm mound, the consumption of wealth in the form of massive bronze hoards and rich grave goods and the use of rock carvings are some features connected to the assumption of an emerging elite in Scandinavia. The Kings and chieftains of Central and Eastern Europe used the trade with copper, tin and gold to create social, economic and political structures. This took place during the end of the third millennium BC but it was not until 500 years later that this process was visible in southern Scandinavia. Bronze was not locally available, and the leading groups were depending on exchange systems and social interaction with the metal producing regions in Eastern and Western Europe (Larsson 1996:7).

When there are apparent links between areas far apart, both in the use of symbols and in depictions, and where trading routes can be traced, one can assume that peoples throughout Europe had connections in various ways. Although the use of marine and inland waterways cannot be attested through finds of boats, the known distribution of objects of stone and metal, the presence of settlements and burials on islands and representations of ships on the rock carvings all suggest that the movement of people and materials was often by sea, and probably easier by sea than by land. The overall distribution of Bronze Age objects and sites tends to be coastal rather than inland, although there are parts of North European area that are isolated from access to marine waterways of the North Sea and the Baltic Sea (Coles & Harding 1979:499). Considering that man colonised the islands east of Australia and New Guinea in the Pacific Ocean 30 000 years ago, journeys of more than 100 kilometres at sea, the thought of going by boat along the shores of western Europe and using the rivers, seems more or less natural. The people making journeys came into contact with different societies and traditions. Travelling to far away places most certainly meant taking risks, and maybe the cultural contacts were not always friendly. This aspect must also be taken into consideration in trying to understand and explain cultural contacts.

The Kula ring in Melanesia, a highly complex exchange system of shell necklaces or "shell money" is an example of exchange of objects with symbolic value only, objects that seem simple and without meaning to us (White 1993). The exchange took place over vast areas to distant places by outrigged canoes decorated with symbolic figures, and the prestige put into and gained from the trade was enormous. Knowledge acquired from these travels was controlled by "specialists" (chiefs or religious leaders) as an attribute and legitimisation of their powers. Those who did not take part in this exchange for various reasons had a lower position in society, and were not seen as "real men". This could be valid also for the chiefs in Bronze Age Scandinavia. The introduction of long distance exchange networks and the occurrence of foreign prestige objects, as well as the knowledge of foreign institutions and religious beliefs meant that certain elite groups could increase their power and status in the society (Kristiansen 1999a: 337f).

Concluding comments

With this presentation I have tried to illuminate and exemplify the complex nature of human interaction and the exchange and transmission of symbols and ideas during the Bronze Age.

I believe that the exchange of objects and the transmission of ideas between southern Scandinavia and the Mediterranean area during the Bronze Age, have been more intense than what is at this point indicated by the archaeological finds. The people of the North were not passive receivers of foreign traditions; the symbols that were integrated in the belief system were carefully picked out and the original meaning was most certainly known and served a special purpose in the society. One of the main purposes with the introduction of foreign symbols into a particular region must have been the acquisition of practices and beliefs related to those specific symbols. The original meaning of the exchanged object was certainly important, and if the regions were exchanging prestige goods or gifts with ritual and sacred meanings in one region, it was most certainly treated as ritual and sacred also in adjacent areas. This might explain why mainly foreign elite, royal or sacred objects and symbols such as parade arms, sun-discs, helmets, etc were imported or copied in South Scandinavia (Larsson 1999:59). It also makes Scandinavia a part of the long-distance trade systems, and offers a different perspective on the profound cultural changes which occurred during the Early Iron Age in Central Europe (Late Bronze Age in Scandinavia) (Wells 1980). It is also important to consider and analyse the relationship between the visible and the invisible flow of objects and knowledge or information, and also what was picked out and what was not. The next step in the investigation must be the development and explication of a general methodology for examining contact situations using archaeological data (e.g. Randsborg 1974; Wells 1980; Kristiansen 1999a).

References

Ahlberg, G.1971. *Fighting on land and and sea in Geometric art.* Skrifter utgivna av svenska institutet i Athen 16. Lund.

Almgren, O. 1927. Hällristningar och kultbruk. Stockholm.

Almgren, B. 1987. *Die Datierung Bronzezeitlicher Felszeichnungen in Westschweden.* Uppsala.

Andersson, G. 1972. Bohusläns hembygdsförenings Årsskrift 1972, p 101.

Bengtsson, L. & Hygen, A. S. 1999. Hällristningar i gränsbygd. Bohuslän och Östfold. Borås.

Bertilsson, U. 1987. The Rock Carvings of Northern Bohuslän. Spatial Structures and Social Symbols. Edsbruk.

1999. Rock Art – divine messages or socio realistic representations? In: Gustafsson, A. & Karlsson, H. (eds.), *Glyfer och rum – en vänbok till Jarl Nordbladh. Pp 743-750.*

Burenhult, G. 1973. Rock Carving Chronology and Rock Carving ships with sails. Meddelende från Lunds Universitets Historiska Museum 1971-72. Lund.

1973. The Rock Carvings of Götaland II. Acta Archaeologica Lundensia 4:8. Lund

1979. *Hällristningar. Hällbilder från sten- och bronsålder.* Malmö Museums utställningskatalog Nr. 330. Malmö.

1980. *Götalands hällristningar.* Del 1. Theses and Papers in North European Archaeology 10. Stockholm.

1999. Arkeologi i Norden 1. Borgå, Finland.

2000. Arkeologi i Norden 2.

Burkert, W. 1985. *Greek Religion.* Harvard University Press.

Casson, L.1991. The Ancient Mariners. Princeton, New Jersey.

Casson, L. 1994. Ships and seafaring in ancient times. London.

Castleden, R. 1991. *Minoans - life in Bronze Age Crete.* New York.

Coles, J. M. & Harding, A. F. 1979. *The Bronze Age in Europe.* London.

Coles, J. 1990. Bilder från forntiden. Uddevalla.

Collis, J. 1989. *The European Iron Age.* London.

Decker, W. 1987. *Sport und spiel im älter Ägypten.* München.

Dickinson, O. T. P. K. 1994. *The Aegean Bronze Age.* Cambridge.

Dietler, M. 1996. Feasts and Commensal Politics in the Political Economy: Food, Power and Status in Prehistoric Europe. I *Food and the Status Quest. An Interdisciplinary Perspective.* Eds. Schiefenhövel, W. & Weissner, P. Providence.

Fredsjö, Å.1971. Hällristningar i Kville. Svenneby socken. Göteborg.

Fredsjö, Å. 1975. Hällristningar i Kville. Bottna socken. Göteborg.

Fridh-Haneson, B-M. 1995. Bronsålder vid Medelhavet. Vad skriftliga källor berättar om den grekiska bronsålderskulturen. In: Håkansson, M. & Engelbrektsson, M. (eds.) *Bohuslän Årsbok 1995. Årgång 17. Pp. 61-82.*

Glob, P. V. 1969. *Helleristninger i Danmark.* Jysk Arkaeologisk selskabs skrifter bind VII.

Halldin, G. 1948. Farkoster från Medelhavets och Västeuropas kuster fram till omkring 500 f. Kr. Sjöhistorisk årsbok 1948. Stockholm.

Higgins, R. 1992. *Minoan and Mycenean Art.* First ed. 1967. London.

Kaul, F. 1995. Ships on Bronzes. I: Crumlin-Pedersen, O. & Much Thye, B. *The Ship as a Symbol in Prehistoric and Medieval Scandinavia.* Papers from an International Research Seminar at the Danish National Museum, Copenhagen, 5th-7th May 1994. Publications from the National Museum. Studies in Arcaeology and History Vol. 1. Köpenhamn.

Kristiansen, K. 1987. Center and periphery in Bronze Age Scandinavia. I *Center and Periphery in the Ancient World.* Eds. Michael Rowlands, Mogens Larsen & Kristian Kristiansen. Cambridge University Press.

1989. Value, ranking and consumption in the Bronze Age. I Nordström, H-Å. & Knape, A. (eds.) *Bronze Age Studies. Transactions of the British-Scandinavian Colloquium in Stockholm, May 10-11, 1985.* The Museum of National Antiquities, Stockholm Studies 6. Stockholm.

1998. *Europe before History.*

1999a. A Theoretical strategy for the interpretation of exchange and interaction in a Bronze Age context. I *L `Atelier du bronzier en Europé du XX du VIII siècle avant notre ère.* Actes du colloque international Bronze '96, Neuchatel et Dijon. III: Production, circulation et consommation du bronze. Paris, CTHS.

1999b. Symbolic structures and social institutions. The twin Rulers in bronze Age Europe. I: (red.) Gustafsson, A. & Karlsson; H. *Glyfer och arkeologiska rum – en vänbok till Jarl Nordbladh.*

Kristiansen, K. & Larsson, T. B. (in prep.). The Great Journey. Symbolic Transmision and Social Transformation in Bronze Age Europe.

Larsson, T. B. 1996. *Kult, Kraft och Kosmos.* Utställningskatalog. Statens Historiska Museum. Stockholm.

1997. *Materiell kultur och religiösa symboler.* Arkeologiska studier vid Umeå Universitet 4. Umeå.

1999. The Transmission of an Élite Ideology. In Goldhahn, J. (ed). *Rock Art as Social Representations.* BAR International Series 794 1999.

Malmer, M.P., 1981. *A chorological study of North European Rock Art.* Kungl. Vitterhets Historie och Antikvitets Akademiens Handlingar. Antikvariska serien 32. Stockholm.

1989. Principles of an non-mythological explanation of North-European Bronze Age Rock Art. I Nordström, H-Å. & Knape, A. (eds.) *Bronze Age Studies. Transactions of the British-Scandinavian Colloquium in Stockholm, May 10-11, 1985.* The Museum of National Antiquities, Stockholm Studies 6. Stockholm.

1992. Weight systems in the Scandinavian Bronze Age. In: *Antiquity, Vol. 66, Nr 251, June 1992, p. 377-388.*

1999. How and why did Greece communicate with Scandinavia in the Bronze Age? In: Orrling, K (ed.) *Communication in Bronze Age Europé. Transactions of the Bronze Age Symposium in Tanumstrand, Bohuslän, Sweden, September 7-10, 1995.* Stockholm.

Mohen, J-P. 1985. Trade Routes. I *The World Atlas of Archaeology.* Ed. Beazley, M. Cambridge.

Morgan, L.1988. The Miniature Wall Paintings of Thera. A Study in Aegan culture and iconography. Cambridge.

Olsson, L. 1996. Skeppets väg till hälleberget. En komparativ bildanalys av hällristningsskepp i Sverige och skeppsbilder från medelhavsområdet. Uppsats i påbyggnadskurs i arkeologi. Stockholms Universitet HT 1996. Stencil.

1997. Med Karon över Styx. En studie av den mediterrana skeppsbildens integrering i den nordiska bronsålderns föreställningsvärld. Magisteruppsats i arkeologi. Stockholms Universitet VT 1997. Stencil.

1998. Med Karon över Styx - skepp som mötas. *Populär Arkeologi Nr. 1 1998.* Hellvi.

1999a. Mediterranean Symbols in Late Bronze Age Rock Art in Southern Scandinavia. I Cruz, A. R. & Oosterbeek, L. *Tomo I. 1° Curso de Arte Pré-Histórica Europeia-1998. Perspectivas em diálogo.* Tomar.

2000. Skepp från Medelhavsområdet på våra hällristningar? I Burenhult, G. (red.) Arkeologi i Norden. Stockholm.

Österholm, S. 1996. Forntidens båtar. Rapport från ett försök med experimentell arkeologi. Hemse.

Pettersson, J. & Kristiansson, G. 1977. *Hällristningar på Tjörn.* Malung.

Randsborg, K. 1974. Social stratification in early bronze Age Denmark: A study on the regulation of Cultural systems. In: Renfrew, C. *The explanation of cultural change.* London.

Randsborg, K. 1996. Absolute Chronology. Archaeological Europé 2500-500 BC. *Acta Archaeologica vol. 67.* 1996.

Stjernquist, B. 1962. Ett praktfynd med sydeuropeiska bronser. *Proxima Thule.* Stockholm.

Wells, P. S. 1980. *Culture contact and culture change. Early iron Age central Europe and the Mediterranean world.* Cambridge.

Westerberg, K. 1983. *Cypriotic ships from the Bronze Age to c. 500 BC.* Göteborg.

White, J. P. 1993. Havens pionjärer. I: Burenhult, G. (red.). *Bra böckers encyclopedi om Människans historia del 2.* Hong Kong.

Zervos, C. 1956. *L'art de la Crète néolithique et minoenne.* Paris.

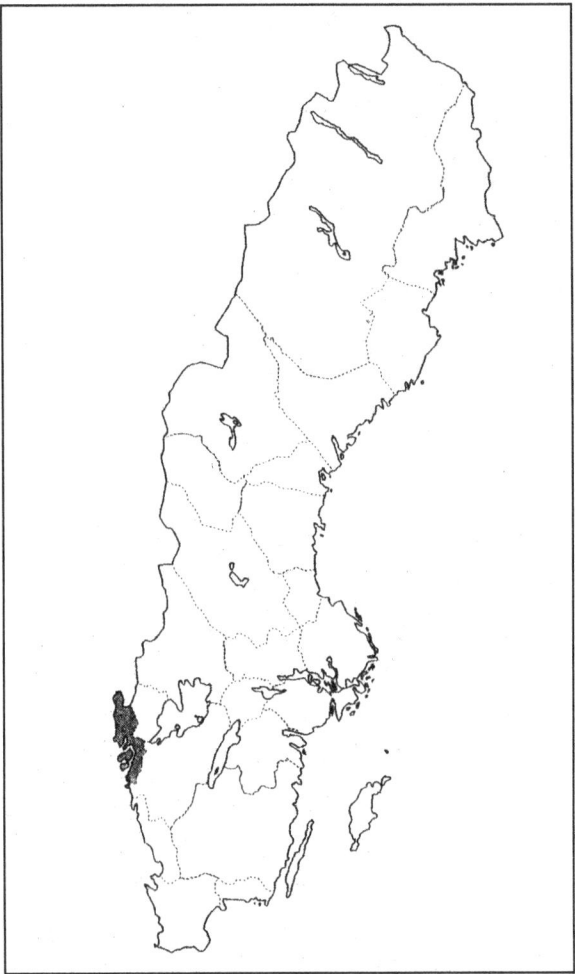

Fig. 1 Map of Sweden with the province of Bohuslän marked. After Bengtsson 1999:310.

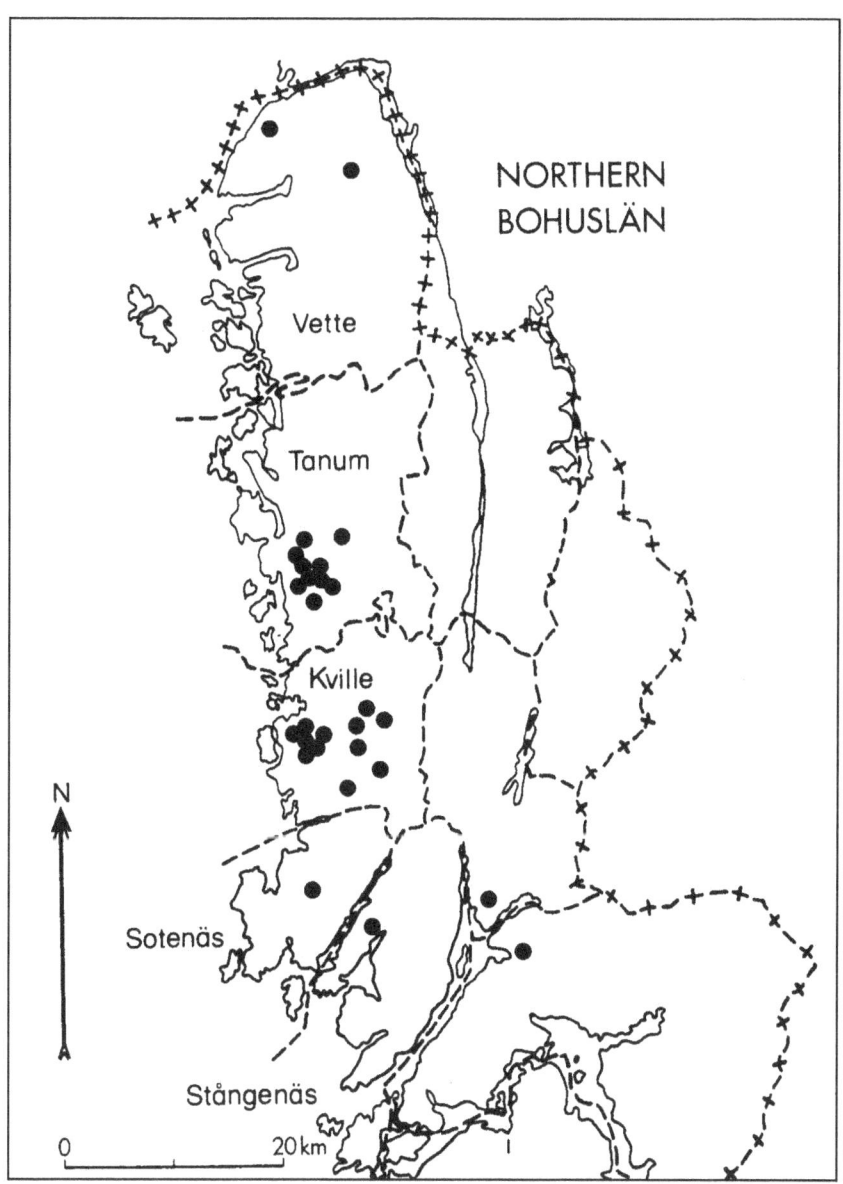

Fig. 2 Map of the larger rock carving areas and localities in Northern Bohuslän. After Bertilsson 1987.

Cultural Interactions in Europe and the Eastern Mediterranean during the Bronze Age (3000-500 BC)

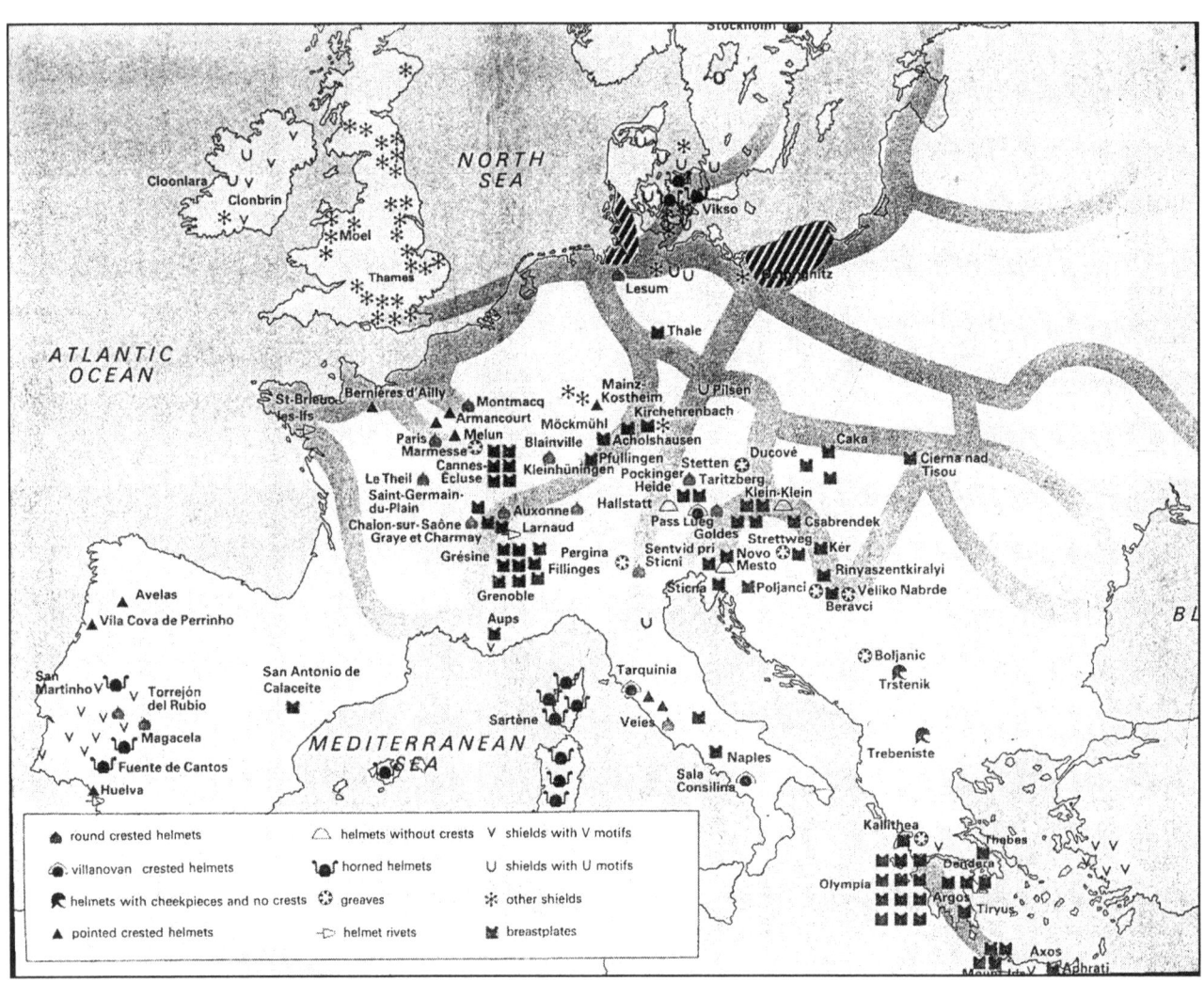

Fig. 3 Map showing links between northern Europe and the Mediterranean area 4000 years ago. The map shows sites where arms dating from the end of the Bronze Age to the beginning of the Iron Age (12th-7th centuries B.C.) have been found, and how Baltic amber spread southwards along certain routes. The bronze parade arms, such as helmets, breastplates, shields and greaves, indicate similar conceptions of warfare and probably also of the system of chiefs. This kind of arms is often decorated with sun and bird motifs, a common feature in Bronze Age Europe. After Mohen 1985.

Fig. 4 Depictions of Scandinavian representations in settings which remind of both Egyptian and Greek religious beliefs, such as the Egyptian grave-paintings and relief images, where votive ships are being offered to the deceased or to the God. (a) A votive ship-carrier from the province of Bohuslän, and (b) from Östergötland. (c) Ritual scene from the Denderah-temple in Egypt, after Burenhult 2000 (d). Ritual votive ceremony depicted on the Hagia Triada sarcophagus from Minoan Crete, after Zervos 1956. (e). Slab no 7 from the Kivik burial mound in the province of Scania in southern Sweden, after Kristianssen 1999.

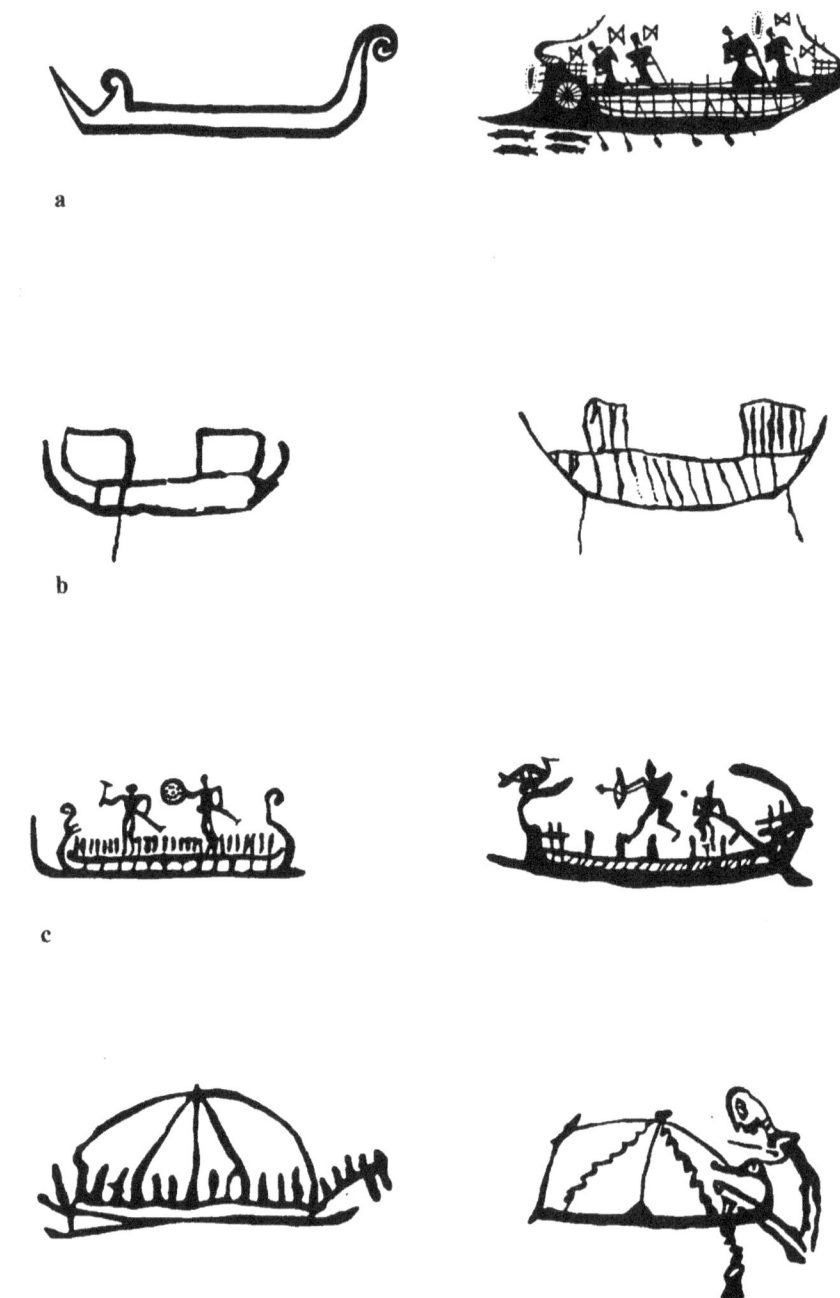

Fig. 5 (a). To the left an example of a Swedish rock carving ship with a massive extension of the keel, perhaps representing a ram. This type of ship engravings shows similarites with vase paintings of Greek wargalleys from the Geometric period, dated around 700 B.C. Right: a Greek galley with a ram and with a similar hull construction and with decorative details turned up- and inwards. Drawing by Li Winter, after Fredsjö 1975; Halldin 1948.
(b). Ship representations with cabins. Left: a rock carving ship from the province of Bohuslän, the only example in Sweden of this type. Right: ship engraved on a mobile block of stone, from Hyria in Greece. The overall shape of the hull, the two cabins and the vertical lines leaping down from the hull are almost identical with the Swedish rock carving ship. Drawing by Li Winter, after Fredsjö 1971; Morgan 1988.
(c). Two representations of a similar warrior scene. Left: a rock carving ship from the province of Bohuslän, equipped with a ram and an extended stern. Two human figures are on the deck, one armed with an axe and a sword with a ferrule, the other with a similar sword and a shield. Right: a vase painting from Eleusis in Greece. Drawing by Li Winter after Coles 1990; Casson 1991.
(d). Rock carving ships with sails are an unusual feature in the South Scandinavian rock carving tradition. It has been disputed whether the art of sailing was known at all during the Bronze age. Left: rock carving ship with mast and strays from the province of Scania in the south of Sweden. Right: Cypriotic vase painting showing a ship with similar details as the ship from Scania, dated to about 700 B.C. Drawing by Li Olsson, after Burenhult 1973; Westerberg 1983.

Fig 6 The Sun-chariot from Trundholm in Denmark, dated to about 1400 BC. After The National Museum of Denmark.

Fig. 7 Acrobats from Scandinavia and the Mediterranean. (a-c) Depictions of bull-leaping ceremonies from Crete, after Higgins 1991; Fridh-Haneson 1995. (d-f) Rock Carving acrobats together with bulls from the province of Bohuslän, after Fredsjö 1975. (g-h) Egyptian female acrobats, after Decker 1987. (i-l) Single representations of acrobats from the province of Bohuslän, after Fredsjö 1971; 1975; Andersson 1972. (m) The only remaining acrobat from the Grevensvænge find from Denmark, after The National Museum of Denmark. (n) Rock Carving ship from Bohuslän, with an acrobat in mid-air, after Burenhult 2000.

Fig. 8 Reconstruction of the bronze figurines in the hoard from Grevensvænge (b) and Faardal (a) in Denmark. After Burenhult 2000.

Cultural Interactions in Europe and the Eastern Mediterranean during the Bronze Age (3000-500 BC)

Fig. 9 Faiance statuette of a Minoan Snake Goddess found in the palace of Knossos in Crete. It is dated to around 1600 BC, after Higgins 1991.

Fig. 10 The cult object from Balkåkra, probably a ritual object connected with sun-worship because of the ten wheel-crosses, interpreted as symbols of the sun. Dated to about 1500 BC, after The National Museum in Stockholm.

The Innovation of Iron.
From Bronze Age to Iron Age Societies in Sweden and Greece.

Eva Hjärthner-Holdar and Christina Risberg

Introduction

Our joint project on the introduction of iron technology in Scandinavia and Greece, financed by the Bank of Sweden Tercentenary Foundation, is an attempt to study the introductory process from the earliest iron objects to the full integration of iron technology into society. We have chosen to study two almost completely different kinds of society in order to understand the mechanisms of technological innovation. The aim of this study is an attempt to relate current theories concerning social systems and structural change with an interpretation of the archaeological material and the results of scientific analyses of archaeometallurgical material.

The introduction of iron technology in different parts of the world has been thoroughly studied (e.g., Wertime & Muhly 1980; Alexander 1980; 1983). The models applied to the introduction of iron technology have so far either had an evolutionary basis built on the conception that you need a long experience of copper and bronze working before attempting to produce iron. The diffusionist perspective sees the Near East in the second millennium BC as the birthplace of iron technology. It is built on a south-north perspective where iron is introduced c. 1200 BC from the Near East to Greece. From there through the Balkans and Italy the technology reaches central and northern Europe and finally Scandinavia and Sweden at a much later date around 500 BC (e.g., Childe 1942, Renfrew 1986; Wertime 1973; Pleiner 1980) (Fig. 1).

Diffusion does not have to be defined in this way since knowledge about a phenomenon does not necessarily lead to an acceptance. There are several delaying mechanisms that come into play and these can vary considerably between individuals and regions (Hägerstrand 1970). This gives us a picture of diffusion that shows a non-linear pattern where iron is introduced and accepted in different regions of Eurasia at different times (Hjärthner-Holdar 1993) (Fig. 2).

Our starting-point is to try to understand the introduction and the role of iron and iron technology within a changing society. The period c. 1200–500 BC is in both Europe and the eastern Mediterranean characterised by fundamental and far-reaching transformations in social structure and economic systems (Rowlands 1984; Snodgrass 1980b; Musti 1991; Ward & Sharp Joukowski 1992; Osborne 1996; Gitin et al. 1998; Kristiansen 1998). We have tried to focus on some issues that we think are crucial to the spread and acceptance of a new technology, in this case iron technology. They include the type of internal social system prevalent in society, external and internal contacts, metallurgical knowledge and know-how, the resource base, i.e., iron ore, fuel and construction material, and the demand, the need, for the new product, iron and steel in this case.

Chronological perspective

The period that we study is c. 1200–700 BC. The absolute dating of the Bronze and Early Iron ages in Europe is the result of a combination of typological methods, historical cross dating and scientific methods, such as radiocarbon dating (^{14}C) and dendrochronology. In Sweden the period studied corresponds to Montelius period III-V (1300–750/700 BC) of the Bronze Age (Kristiansen 1998; Randsborg 1996; Vankilde 1996; Harding 2000). Traditionally the beginning of the Iron Age in Sweden is set around 500 BC.

In Greece the period 1200–700 comprises the end of the Bronze Age and the beginning of the Iron Age. Traditionally the dividing line between Bronze Age and the Early Iron Age is around 1050/1025 BC and is based on changes in Attic pottery styles. Apart from the problem of deciding the criteria for a division between the Bronze Age and the Iron Age there are considerable regional variations to take into consideration (Desborough 1952; Snodgrass 1971, 106-136; Warren & Hankey 1989; Mountjoy 1993; 1999, 16f, 38-41).

Social structure

To understand how iron technology is introduced and accepted a study of the social system of the receiving area is needed. Besides the basic requirements for producing iron, ore, fuel etc. the social system must be constructed so that it allows production and use of iron to satisfy the need for metal. The most important factor seems to be that society is decentralised with little or no central authority and where the old elites that built their power on the acquisition and control of bronze no longer exist or function as they did before. Perhaps a more complex course of events should be envisioned in parts of the Near East where iron seems to have been introduced during a period when the old empires were in crisis and before the new ones were formed (Pigott 1982).

In our project we have been working with the concept of simple and complex chiefdoms since this is, in our view, most compatible with the historical situation (Earle 1991; 1997; Stein & Rothman 1994).

Sweden

Most parts of southern Sweden, are characterised by simple chiefdoms, small independent units with some regional co-operation (Fig. 3). Society was characterised by a stable settlement pattern which could be due to that there were neither social nor ecological over exploitation and new land that could be used for new settlements was raised from the sea (Hjärthner-Holdar 1989:109ff; Jensen 1989:115ff). There are, however, in the beginning of the period, some profound changes in architecture, family structure and funeral ritual. The architecture changes from large communal houses to smaller houses probably intended for family groups (Göthberg et. al. 1995). The funeral rites change from inhumation to cremation. These societies were manufacturing and using bronze but the power stability was not dependent on it. In clear contrast to the situation in Sweden Denmark was during this period characterised by more complex chiefdoms with competitive power structures, which had monopolised the exchange of prestige gods and the flow of bronze. At the same time this also made the structure dependent on the flow and exchange of bronze and precious metals in the elite networks (Kristiansen 1993:143ff; 1998). This structure seems to have been in existence even during the late phase of period VI (Thrane 1993:79ff). If the system, as it seems to have done in for example Denmark, can support and keep the people satisfied then nothing will happen. But when the system cannot support its members changes will appear. In Denmark a regionalisation took place at the end of the Bronze Age and a number of new power constellations appeared in the earliest phase (Period I). of the Iron Age (e.g., Becker 1961). This led to an increase in the metal that was needed and this could favour the introduction of a new technology and the use of a local resource – in this case iron ore. In Sweden the power structure never became very advanced and had the possibility to monopolise the exchange of prestige goods and the flow of bronze. The decentralised power structure, the external interactions, the transmission of know-how and the resources to exploit the new technology made it possible to introduce and get an acceptance for iron technology. A more thorough study of the different power structures can perhaps help to explain the different modes of introduction in the two areas.

Greece

The Bronze Age
During period c. 1200–700 BC mainland Greece seem to consist of small, decentralised chiefdoms with no or very limited central authority. There are however regional differences between probably quite complex systems in some areas in central and southern Greece compared to other more marginal areas (Snodgrass 1971; Whitley 1991; Morris 1997).

This is in clear contrast to the previous period, c. 1400–1200, or using pottery designations, the Late Helladic IIIA-IIIB periods, when the Mycenaean system was in function. This was a hierarchical system built on centralised power in a limited number of so-called palace sites. These palace structures are recognised by their use of monumental architecture with a so-called *megaron* as a central unit, and a sophisticated administrative system built on the use of written documents. Characteristic was also a distinct social hierarchy which can be seen in the use of stratified graves, religious rituals and iconography and exchanges with wide areas of the Mediterranean (Shelmerdine 1997, 557-563). The palaces were, with the purpose of having access to prestige and luxury commodities, involved in strategic areas of agricultural production and manufacture of craft goods but exercised only partial control of the economic activity in their territories (Halstead 1992; Foxhall 1995; Shelmerdine 1997; 1999).

Our knowledge of the social structure of the Mycenaean palaces and their economy is to a large extent based on the administrative texts preserved on the Linear B tablets found both on Crete and the mainland (Deger-Jalkotzy 1983b; Hooker 1987a, b; 1995; Palaima 1990). These are written in Greek and dated c. 1300–1200 BC, with a main period during the second half of the 13th century (Hooker 1980; Palaima 1988; Bennet 1997). The social hierarchy of Mycenaean society evident from the Linear B tablets show several different levels of authority from the king, the *vanax*, down to leaders on a local level (Shelmerdine 1997; Bennet 1997) and the *damos*, a collective that can perhaps be translated as village (Lejeune 1965; Palmer 1984).

Around 1200, in the Late Helladic IIIB2 period, this system is weakened by the destruction of many palace sites and severe demographic changes and eventually disappears during the last Bronze Age period, the Late Helladic IIIC period. There are various explanations why this system was transformed, or met with catastrophes so severe that it could not be reconstructed. These include theories based on internal economic factors such as the disruption of trade in the eastern Mediterranean owing to the Sea Peoples, or that the Mycenaean economy was too specialised to withstand 'stress'. Other causes include invasion, natural catastrophes, internal warfare and social unrest (Deger-Jalkotzy 1991; 1996). A change in military tactics and a shift from chariot warfare to light-armed infantry has also been suggested as a cause for the collapse (Drews 1993).

Suffice to say that the disruption of the palace system causes destruction, population movements and a period of general unrest which leads ultimately to a restructuring of Greek society during the following Late Helladic III C and Early Iron Age periods. More recent research shows that the traditional view of a society in severe decline during the post-palatial phase is not necessarily the case and some changes may even have been of a positive character (Deger-Jalkotzy 1998; Small 1998). The final result is an economy based on subsistence farming in household units, the *oikos*. What we see is not a complete breakdown of the social order but a society organised on a different scale where pre-existing values and structures are transformed. In some respects the status of local elites and their ability to control local resources grew (Foxhall 1995; Deger-Jalkotzy 1998; Small 1998).

During the first phase, Late Helladic III C early, a partial recovery took place and although many sites were abandoned other settlements, especially in the islands, continued to be in use. During this period some new features that were introduced already during the preceding period become much more common; these include the violin bow fibula, the Naue II sword (Snodgrass 1974; Vanschoonwinkel 1991) and hand-made burnished pottery (Rutter 1975; 1990; Deger-Jalkotzy 1983a; Small 1990; 1997).

During the following phase, III C Middle, the local production of pottery was of a high quality (Mountjoy 1993; 1999) and some of the palaces, notably Mycenae and Tiryns, were still partly occupied and these, and other settlements, probably functioned as centres of a local power (Deger-Jalkotzy 1998). This second phase ends with further destruction at some of the still occupied palace sites and several other settlements were abandoned leading to depopulation in some areas (Deger-Jalkotzy 1998).

The last phase of the Late Helladic III C Late, sees several changes in many areas although habitation continues at some Mycenaean sites; the locally produced pottery disappears and the hand-made burnished ware becomes more common (Mountjoy 1993; 1999).

The general picture of the Mycenaean mainland by the middle of the 11th century is one of demographic changes, depopulation evidenced in the abandonment of settlements and practical desertion of some areas. A change in culture is evident in pottery style, in dress and burial practice (Desborough 1964; 1972; Snodgrass 1971; Vanschoonwinkel 1991; Mazarakis Ainian 1997).

Remains from the second half of the 11th century, the Submycenaean period, are very scanty and consist primarily of tomb material. The arched fibulae, the long dress pins and single burials, both in cremation and inhumation, appear (Deger-Jalkotzy 1998). The pottery defined as Submycenaean is very diverse and in some instances difficult to identify (Mountjoy 1993; 1999). This has led some scholars to dispute this as a separate phase and preferring to see Submycenaean pottery as contemporaneous with the late phase of III C (Rutter 1978) while other maintain the validity of Submycenaean as a separate phase (Mountjoy 1988; Deger-Jalkotzy 1998).

The Iron Age
Earlier research on the early Iron Age, the so-called Dark Age, has generally emphasised the discontinuity and the poverty of the material culture and the interruption of both the internal and external contacts and exchanges (Snodgrass 1971; Desborough 1972; Coldstream 1977; Morris 1997). More recent research, however, underscores the continuity in material culture and social structure with the Bronze Age and especially the Late Helladic III C period (Deger-Jalkotzy 1998; Small 1998). Some scholars maintain that the term 'Dark Age' should perhaps be abandoned altogether (Papadopoulos 1993; 1996).

There is considerable controversy on the structure of society during the early Iron Age. It is usually portrayed as egalitarian or at least relatively unstratified and the political power restricted to each individual settlement (Snodgrass 1987). Others prefer to see a more hierarchical society where each settlement had their own leading men, be it king, chief or big man (Qviller 1981; Donlan 1985; 1989). The term *basileus*, probably with roots in early Mycenaean society, survives the transformations at the end of the Bronze Age and in the Homeric epics this is the name of the local leaders, the kings (Drews 1983; Carlier 1995; Palaima 1995; Lejdegård 1998; Shelmerdine 1997; Bennet 1997). The main characteristic of Iron Age society seems to be the diversity in material culture and social relations (Morris 1997; Whitley 1991). Towards the end of the 10th century conditions seem to change in parts of Greece and there are signs of a growth in overseas exchanges and an expansion of settlements (Morris 1997; Sherratt & Sherratt 1993), using pre-existing trade routes (Bennet 1997). During the 8th century the changes, in some areas, become much more pronounced, even dramatic. The population increases to larger communities and political centralisation leading ultimately to urbanisation and state formation, the *polis* (Snodgrass 1980; 1993). Other significant results are that regional differences are lessened, new settlements and colonies abroad are founded, the traded goods become more diverse and frequent (Morris 1997; Sherratt & Sherratt 1993; Foxhall 1998) and the alphabet is introduced from the eastern Mediterranean (Coldstream 1977).

The introduction of iron technology

Iron objects had been in circulation in high status contexts in Egypt and Middle East since the 4th millennium BC (Waldbaum 1978) when around 1200 the iron and iron technology appeared in Sweden. To Sweden iron technology comes more or less as a package. There seems to be no stage with only imported iron objects belonging to the elite. Finished objects, iron production and forging all appear at the same time. What is also important in this case is that iron is from the beginning used for tools and weapons and they were made of good iron qualities like carbon steel and phosphorous iron. This also means that there were only small amounts of slag inclusions in the iron and that the smiths could produce different qualities, like ferrite, carbon steel and phosphorus iron, that were adapted to their future uses like steel for edges in tools. Iron ore, fuel and building material for furnaces are easily found in Sweden. The production of iron does not seem to appear only in what might be considered to be elite settlements (Hjärthner-Holdar 1993). Lars Nørbach from the University of Aarhus in Denmark has studied the earliest finds of iron production in Denmark. The results of the investigation was that there is no sign of iron production or even the use of imported iron objects in Denmark before M VI except for the fragment of an iron knife from Grødeby on Bornholm (Nørbach 1998:53ff; Vedel 1886:262). Iron ores are quite easily obtained in

Denmark so there is no lack of raw material for iron production.

This fact leads to a modification of previous interpretations of patterns of diffusion. It must be other contacts and maybe also the power system that led to the early acceptance of iron technology in Sweden. It is also highly likely that knowledge of iron technology came about in the interaction with the areas east of Sweden, i. e., Russia, not in the contacts with areas to the south-west (Hjärthner-Holdar 1993).

One problem that is of virtual importance in this case is the transmission of this knowledge. To be able to transform knowledge generally the two parties must be both socially and culturally equal and the systems must be compatible. Eastern and Northern Sweden have had contacts to the east for a long period of time before this event and therefor there probably were alliances already built up and ready to be used (Tallgren 1916; 1937). This is an issue that this project will continue to work with.

If we look at Sweden in more detail there will of course be differences in the time schedule of the introduction in different regions (Fig. 4). But in a North East to South West direction the introduction and acceptance of iron technology takes place in the first half of the period studied. The spread of iron technology and production concentrated on tools leads to the conclusion that the Iron Age in Sweden begins somewhere around 750–700 BC. Oscar Montelius suggested this already in the beginning of the 20th century (Montelius 1913). This is also supported by the fact that the material attributed to period VI of the Bronze Age consists more or less only of ornaments made of bronze.

Metalworking, viz. bronze, has by the end of the Bronze Age a long tradition in Greece and especially so during the Late Bronze Age. Objects in iron are not unknown either. From around the 17th century and with an increase after c. 1200, objects, esp. prestige objects, jewellery and ornaments, but also some functional tools, reached Minoan and Mycenaean Greece (Iakovides 1970; Waldbaum 1978; 1980; Varoufakis 1983; 1989). Some of the early rings are probably manufactured in Greece (Waldbaum 1978; 1980; Vanschoonwinkel 1991).

The model proposed by Anthony Snodgrass divides the introduction of iron technology into three phases. The first phase is the longest with a few items imported to Greece during the 2nd millennium. The second, and much shorter, phase starts around 1200 with the first functional tools and weapons; iron knives with bronze rivets, swords, lances and daggers (Waldbaum 1983). Bronze is still used for other types of artefacts. The third phase, from around 1050, sees the full use of iron in central parts of Greece when iron technology was introduced from Cyprus. The main reason for the adoption is the lack of access to resources of tin and copper after the rupture of long-distance trade leading to a need to exploit local sources of iron (Snodgrass 1971; 1980a; 1983; 1989). It is almost generally agreed that iron technology reached central Greece from Cyprus although the available evidence is far from conclusive (Vanschoonwinkel 1991; Waldbaum 1983; 1989).

Resources of iron ore are available in many parts of Greece (Snodgrass 1989; Varoufakis 1989). It is however difficult to know when these sources were first used. A part of our project is aimed at studying resources of iron ore in Argolis and Ermione in the Peloponnese. This is to investigate possible local sources used for iron production in Asine during the Early Iron Age (Backe-Forsberg & Risberg 1986; Backe-Forsberg & Risberg in press; Backe-Forsberg et al. in press; Backe-Forsberg et al. forthcoming). Other areas that have been or are being studied at the moment include northern Greece, esp. Macedonia and Thrace, areas that have perhaps the richest sources of iron ore (Photos 1987), Crete and the Cycladic islands. In all of these areas early iron objects have been found dating to the introductory phase, 1200–900 BC (Snodgrass 1971; 1983; 1989; Sherratt 1994; Risberg forthcoming) (Fig. 5).

Cultural interaction, innovation theories and know-how

Sweden

The Mälar Valley is an interaction zone with contacts in all directions. Different types of artefacts confirm this, striated pottery (Fig. 6) and the textile impressed ware tradition come from the east. The pots themselves are not imported but made in Sweden. Analyses made so far on the pots show that they are made from local clay (Lindahl 1992). Also from the east come different types of bronze artefacts, like the Mälardalen celts (Fig. 7). They clearly originate from the east, there are at least 265 celts of this type found in graves in Russia where they are called *Akosinsko-Melarski* celts (Fig. 6) (Chalikov 1977:123ff, fig 46, 47; Patrousjev 1984:64ff, fig 36). As part of our project six Mälaradalen celts found in Sweden have been analysed. The chemical analyses showed that we are dealing with original metal and not re-melted scrap. One of the celts was analysed with lead isotope analysis (LIA). The result showed that the best isotopic and regional and geological match is to be found in the western foreland of the Ural Mountains (Kresten 2000). This is also in accordance with the archaeological findings. Other examples of imported phenomena are the Lausitz pottery tradition and Hallstatt bronzes from the south as well as Nordic bronzes and a Nordic architectural tradition show that Sweden belongs to the area of the Nordic Bronze Age. The architecture also connects us to the North West European tradition. The funerary ritual is influenced by the Urnfield tradition.

During this period Europe seems to be divided into an eastern and a western part. In this perspective at least Eastern Sweden also belongs to the eastern part like for example also Bornholm. For example there is a hoard consisting of 16 Mälardalen celts found on Bornholm (Baudou 1960:174). The rest of Denmark belongs to the western part. In the east iron technology is accepted at an early stage while the acceptance of the iron technology is slower in the west and the high status bronze production moves west. This might be due to the situation in central Asia where iron have been used as early as 2500 BC in for example the Pit Grave (Yamnaya) culture and by the Catacomb as early as early as 1800 BC (Shramko 1990; Morgunova & Kravtsov 1994). Due both to internal and external factors there were movements in the east that also affected the eastern parts of Europe. Perhaps that was one of the factors that put an end to the Hungarian bronze workshops and could also be one of the factors that led to the introduction of iron technology.

Greece

The area of contact both within the Aegean and surrounding areas are clearly diminished during the early phase of the Iron Age compared to the previous Late Bronze Age period. Contacts have not, however, been completely ruptured and a new period of external contacts starts probably already around 1000–900 BC (Sherratt & Sherratt 1993).

It is clear that southern and central Greece during this period has an eastern direction of its main contacts, through the Aegean islands, including Crete and then on to Cyprus. Many scholars take it almost as a proven fact that the introduction of iron technology to these areas in Greece must indeed have come from Cyprus (Snodgrass 1971; 1983; 1989; Vanschoonwinkel 1991).

During the period 1200–c. 800/750 the northern parts of Greece, Macedonia and Thrace in particular, seems to have had almost no contact with the southern parts. There are few exceptions to this pattern and only a few areas, mainly coastal, continue to interact with southern Greece (Morris 1997). It is therefore not conceivable that the technology was introduced from the south. It must have reached northern Greece another way (Snodgrass 1971; Photos 1987).

Conclusion

One important conclusion that we can draw at this stage in our work is that perhaps the most important factor affecting the introduction of iron, beside access to raw material and technological knowledge, is the existence of a social system that in order to satisfy a need for metal allows the production and use of iron. This is a decentralised society with no or only limited central control and where old elites, founding the control on access to bronze, no longer exist or have ceased to function.

There are fundamental differences between our study areas but there are also quite a number of similarities. During the period c. 1200–700 BC both areas seems to have the similar conditions such as:

Decentralised, small simple chiefdoms with little or no central administration or control.

Interactions with large areas in all directions both internally and externally.

Resources to exploit the new technology – both know-how and plenty of scattered iron ore sources and fuel.

A need of metal, which could not be met by the import and or production of bronze – we are talking about an increased demand/enhanced demand not a decrease in availability.

People in both areas very quickly saw the advantage i.e., that iron was a god metal for working tools and weapons and they quickly learnt how to produce good iron qualities like for example carbon steel. The conclusions so far will be that the introduction and acceptance is dependent on the internal structure, the external contacts and the transmission of knowledge and know-how. The decentralised power structure, the external interactions, the transmission of know-how and the resources to exploit the new technology made it possible to introduce and get an acceptance for iron technology.

References

Alexander, J.A. 1980. The spread and development of iron using in Europe and Africa. In *Proceedings of the 8th Panafrican Congress of Prehistory and Quarternary Studies. Nairobi 5-10 September 1977*, eds. R.E. Leakey & B.A.Ogot, Nairobi, 327-330.

1983. Some neglected factors in the spread of iron-using. In *Festschrift für Hans Hingst zum 75 Geburtstag*, (OFFA 40), Neumünster, 29-33.

Backe-Forsberg, Y. & Risberg, C. 1986. Metal working at Asine. "New" finds from the 1926 season. *OpAth* 15, 123-125.

in press. Archaeometallurgical Methods Applied to Remains of Iron Production from the Geometric Period at Asine. In *New research on old material. Studies in material from the old Swedish excavations at Asine and Berbati in celebration of the 50th anniversary of the Swedish Institute at Athens, May 1998*, (ActaAth-8°, 17), ed. B. Wells.

& Y. Bassiakos. *in press*. Metal working at Asine. Report on the remains of iron production from the Barbouna area and the area East of the Acropolis. *OpAth*.

& Y. Bassiakos. *forthcoming*. Metal working at Asine. Report on the remains of iron production from the Lower Town. *Asine III. Supplemetary Studies on the Swedish Excavations 1922-1930*, 2, eds. R. Hägg, G.C. Nordquist & B. Wells.

Baudou, E. 1960. *Die regionale und chronologische Einteilung der jüngeren Bronzezeit im Nordischen Kreis*. Stockholm.

Becker, C.J. 1961, *Førromersk Jernalder i Syd- og Midjylland*, København.

Bennet, J. 1997. Homer and the Bronze Age. In *A New Companion to Homer* (Mnemosyne suppl. 163), eds. B. Powell & I. Morris, Leiden, 511-533.

Carlier, P. 1995. Qa-si-re-u et qa-si-re-wi-ja. In *Politeia: Society and State in the Aegean Bronze Age. Proceedings of the 5th International Aegean Conference / 5e Rencontre égéenne internationale, University of Heidelberg, Archäologisches Institut, 10-13 April 1994*, II., eds., R. Laffineur & W.-D. Niemeier, (Aegaeum 12), Liège & Austin, 355-364.

Chalikov, A. Ch. 1977. *Volga-Kamije v nacale epochi rannego zjeleza* (VIII–VI vv N E). Akademija Nauk SSSR. Moskva.

Childe, V.G.1942. *Archaeological ages as technological stages* (Journal of the Royal Anthropological Institute of Great Britain and Ireland, 74). London.

Coldstream, J.N. 1977. *Geometric Greece*. London.

Deger-Jalkotzy, S. 1983a. Das Problem der 'Handmade Burnished Ware'. In *Griechenland, die Ägäis und die Levante während der 'Dark Ages' vom 12. bis zum 9. Jahrhundert v.Chr. Symposion von Stift Zwettl (Niederösterreich), 11-14 Oktober 1980*, ed. S. Deger-Jalkotzy (Kommission für mykenische Forschung 10. SBWien 418), Wien, 161-168.

1983b. Zum Charakter und zur Herausbildung der mykenischen Sozialstruktur. In *Res Mycenaeae. Akten de VII. Internationalen Mykenologischen Colloquiums in Nürnberg vom 6.-10. April 1981*, eds. A. Heubeck & G. Neumann, Göttingen, 89-111.

1991. Die Erforschung des Zusammanebruchs der sogennanten mykenischen Welt und der sogennanten dunklen Jahrhunderte. In *Zweihundert Jahre Homer, Colloquium Rauricum II, Augst bei Basel 1989*, ed. J. Latacz, Stuttgart & Leipzig, 127-154.

1996. On the Negative Aspects of the Mycenaean Palace System. In *Atti e memorie del secondo Congresso internazionale di micenologia, Roma-Napoli, 14-20 ottobre 1991*, 2, eds. E. De Miro, L. Godart & A. Sacconi, Rome, 715-728.

1998. The Last Mycenaeans and their Successors Updated. In *Mediterranean Peoples in Transition: Thirteenth to Early Tenth Centuries BCE. In Honour of Professor Trude Dothan*, eds. S. Gitin, A. Mazar & E. Stern, Jerusalem, 114-128.

Desborough, V. R. d'A. 1952. *Protogeometric pottery*. Oxford.

1964. *The Last Mycenaeans and their successors*. Oxford.

1972. *The Greek Dark Ages*. London.

Donlan, W. 1985. The social groups of DA Greece. *CP* 80: 293-308.

1989. The pre-state community in Greece. *SymbOslo* 64: 5-29.

Drews, R. 1983. *Basileus: The Evidence for Kingship in Geometric Greece*. New Haven.

1993. *End of the Bronze Age: Changes in Warfare and the Catastrophe ca. 1200 BC*. Princeton.

Earle, T. 1991, ed. *Chiefdoms: power, economy and ideology*. Cambridge.

1997. *How Chiefs Come to Power*. Stanford, CA.

Foxhall, L. 1995. Bronze to iron: agricultural systems and political structures in Late Bronze Age and Early Iron Age Greece. *BSA* 90: 239-250.

1998. Cargoes of Heart's Desire. The character of trade in the archaic Greek world. In *Archaic Greece: New Approaches and New Evidence*, eds. N. Fisher & H. van Wees, London, 295-309.

Gitin, S., Mazar, A. &Stern, E. 1998. *Mediterranean peoples in transition: thirteenth to early tenth centuries BCE: in honour of Professor Trude Dothan*. Jerusalem.

Göthberg, H. Kyhlberg, O. & Vinberg, A. 1995. *Hus och Gård. Hus och gård i det förurbana samhället – Rapport från ett sektorsforskningsprojekt vid Riksantikvarieämbetet* (Riksantikvarieämbetet, Arkeologiska undersökningar. Skrifter nr 14). Stockholm.

Halstead, P. 1992. The Mycenaean Palatial Economy: Making the most of the gaps in the Evidence. *PCPS* 38, 57-86.

Harding, A.F. 2000. *European societies in the Bronze Age*. Cambridge.

Hjärthner-Holdar, E. 1989. Bebyggelseutvecklingen kring en viktig kommunikationsled i Trögd. In *Arkeologi på väg. Undersökningar för E18 Enköping-Bålsta*. Riksantikvarieämbetet (Byrån för arkeologiska undersökningar), Stockholm.

1993. *Järnets och järnmetallurgins introduktion i Sverige* (Aun 16). Uppsala.

Hooker, J. T. 1980. *Linear B: an introduction*. Bristol.

1987a. Minoan and Mycenaean Administration: A Comparison of the Knossos and Pylos Archives. In *The Function of the Minoan Palaces. Proceedings of the Fourth International Symposium at the Swedish Institute in Athens, 10-16 June, 1984*, eds. R. Hägg & N. Marinatos, (S.I.A, 4°, 35), Stockholm, 313-316.

1987b. Titles and Functions in the Pylian State. In *Studies in Mycenaean and Classical Greek Presented to John Chadwick*, eds. J.T. Killen, J.L, Melena & J.-P. Olivier, (Minos 20-22), Salamanca, 257-268.

1995. Linear B as a Source for Social History. In *The Greek World*, ed. A. Powell, London, 7-26.

Hägerstrand, T. 1970. *Innovation diffusion as a spatial process*. Lund.

Iakovides, S. 1970. He emfanisis tou siderou eis tin Ellada. *AAA* 3, 288-296.

Jensen, R. 1989. Bosättning och ekonomi – Inomregionala differenser i Mälardalen. In *Regionale forhold i nordisk Bronzealder. 5. Nordiske Symposium for Bronzealderforskning på Sandbjerg slot 1987*, ed. Jens Poulsen, (Jysk Arkæologisk Selskabs Skrifter XXIV). Århus.

Kresten, P. 2000. *Analysis of LBA celts from the colletions of the Museum of Nordic Antiquities, University of Uppsala. Project " Iron technology – a successful innovation. From bronze to iron in Scandinavia and Greece"*, (Research Report R0005. National Heritage Board, Geoarchaeological Laboratory). Uppsala

Kristiansen, K. 1993. From Villanova to Seddin. Reconstruction of an Elite Exchange Network during the Eighth Century BC. In *Trade and Exchange in Prehistoric Europe*, ed. Ch. Scarre & F. Healy, Oxford.

1998. *Europe before history*. Cambridge.

Lejdegård, H. 1998. The function and social position of the Mycenaean QA-SI-RE-U. *Minos*, 31-32, 1996-97, 371-378.

Lejeune, M. 1965. Le DAMOS dans la société mycénienne. *REG* 78, 1-22

Lindahl, A. 1992. Analys av strimmig och textilintryckt keramik från ett gravfält i Mälardalen. *KFL Rapport* 1992. Lund.

Mazarakis Ainian, A. 1997. *From rulers' dwellings to temples. Architecture, religion and society in Early Iron Age Greece (1100-700 B.C.)*. Jonsered.

Montelius, O. 1913. När började man allmänt använda järn? *Fornvännen* årg 8.

Morgunova, N.L. & Kravstov, A.J. 1994. *Pamjatniki drevnejanoj kultury na ileke. Akademija nauk*. Ekaterinburg.

Morris, I. 1997. Homer and the Iron Age. In *A New Companion to Homer* (Mnemosyne suppl. 163), eds. B. Powell & I. Morris, Leiden, 535-559.

Mountjoy, P.A. 1988. LHIIIC Late versus Submycenaean: The Kerameikos Pompeion Cemetery Reviewed. *BICS* 35, 174-177.

1993. *Mycenaean Pottery: an introduction*. Oxford.

1999. *Regional Mycenaean decorated pottery*. I-II. Leidorf.

Musti, D. ed. 1991. *La transizione dal Miceneo all'Alto Arcaismo: dal palazzo alla città: Atti del convegno internazionale, Roma, 14-19 marzo 1988*. Roma.

Nørbach, L. Ch. 1998. *Ironworking in Denmark. From the Late Bronze Age to the Early Roman Iron Age* (Acta Archaeologica 69). København.

Osborne, R. 1996. *Greece in the making, 1200-479 BC.* London.

Palaima, T.G. 1988. The Development of the Mycenaean Writing System. *MINOS Suppl.* 10, 269-342.

1990. Origin, Development, Transition and Transformation: the Purposes and Techniques of Administration in Minoan and Mycenaean Society. In *Aegean Seals, Sealings and Administration. Proceedings of the NEH-Dickson Conference of the Program in Aegean Scripts and Prehistory of the Department of Classics, University of Texas at Austin, January 11-13, 1989*, ed., T.G. Palaima (Aegaeum 5), Liège, 83-104.

1995. The Nature of the Mycenaean *Wanax*: Non-Indo-European Origins and Priestly Functions. In *The Role of the Ruler in the Prehistoric Aegean : Proceedings of a Panel Discussion Presented at the Annual Meeting of the Archaeological Institute of America, New Orleans, Louisiana 28 December 1992* (Aegaeum 11), ed. P. Rehak, Liège & Austin, 119-139.

Palmer, L.R. 1984. The Mycenaean Palace and the Damos. In *Aux origines de l'Hellénisme. La Crète et la Grèce. Hommage à Henri van Effenterre présenté par le Centre G. Glotz*, Paris, 151-159.

Papadopoulos, J.K. 1993. To Kill a Cemetery: The Athenian Kerameikos and the Early Iron Age in the Aegean. *MeditArch* 6, 175-206.

1996. Dark Age Greece. In *Oxford Companion to Archaeology*, Oxford, 253-255.

Patrousjev, V.S. 1984. Marijkij Kraj v VII–VI vv do n. e. Starsjij Achmylovskij Mogilnik', *Josjkar-Ola*. Moskva.

Photos, E. 1987. *Early Extractive Iron metallurgy in N Greece: a unified approach to regional archaeometallurgy*. Diss. University of London.

Pigott, V.C. 1982. The Innovation of Iron: Cultural Dynamics in Technological Change. *Expedition* 24/25, 20-25.

Pleiner, R. 1980. Early iron metallurgy in Europé. In *The Coming of the Age of Iron*, eds. T. Wertime & J.D. Muhly, New Haven, 375-425.

Qviller, B. 1981. The dynamics of the Homeric society. *SymbOslo* 56, 109-155.

Randsborg, K. ed. 1996. *Absolute Chronology. Arcaheological Europe 2500-500 BC*. København.

Renfrew, C. 1986. Varna and the emergence of wealth in prehistoric Europe. In *The social life of things: Commodities in cultural perspective*, ed. A. Appadurai, Cambridge, 141-168.

1996. Who were the Minoans? Towards a population history of Crete. *Cretan Studies* 5, 1-27.

Risberg, C. *forthcoming*. The Early Iron Age in Greece - Myth or Reality? In *Early Ironworking in Europe. Archaeology and Experiment. International Conference at Plas Tan y Bwlch, Wales 19-25/9 1997*, eds. P. & S. Crew.

Rowlands, M.J. 1984. Conceptualizing the European Bronze and early Iron Age. In *European social evolution*, ed. J. Bintliff, Bradford, 147-156.

Rutter, J. B. 1975. Ceramic Evidence for Northern Intruders in Southern Greece at the Beginning of the Late Helladic IIIC Period. *AJA* 79, 17-32.

1978. A Plea for the Abandonment of the Term 'Submycenaean'. *TUAS* 3, 58-65.

1990. Some Comments on Interpreting the Dark-surfaced Handmade Burnished Pottery of the 13th and 12th Century B.C. Aegean. *JMA* 3, 29-49.

Shelmerdine, C.W. 1997. Review of Aegean Prehistory VI: The Palatial Bronze Age of the Southern and Central Greek Mainland. *AJA* 101, 537-585.

1999. Administration in the Mycenaean Palaces: Where's the Chief? In *Rethinking Mycenaean Palaces: New Interpretations of an Old Idea*, eds. M.L. Galaty & W.A. Parkinson, Los Angeles, 19-24.

Sherratt, A. & Sherratt, E.S. 1993. The growth of the Mediterranean economy in the early first millenium BC. *WorldArch* 24, 361-378.

Sherratt, E.S. 1994. Commerce, iron and ideology: Metallurgical innovation in 12th-11th century Cyprus. In *Proceedings of the International Symposium Cyprus in the 11th century BC*, ed. V. Karageorghis, Nicosia, 59-106.

Shramko, B.A. 1990. Eine Studie zum eisernen Dolch der Frühbronzezeit aus Grabhügel bei Gerasimovka. Paper delivered at *Symposium international du Comité pour la Sidérurgie Ancienne: Paleometallurgie du fer et cultures, Belfort, France, Novembre 1990*.

Small, D.B. 1990. Handmade Burnished Ware and Prehistoric Aegean Economics: An Argument for Indigenous Appearance. *JMA* 3, 3-25.

1997. Can We Move Forward? Comments on the Current Debate over Handmade Burnished Ware. *JMA* 10, 223-228.

1998. Surviving the Collapse: The Oikos and Structural Continuity between Late Bronze Age and Later Greece. In *Mediterranean Peoples in Transition: Thirteenth to Early Tenth Centuries BCE. In Honor of Professor Trude Dothan*, eds. S. Gitin, A. Mazar & E. Stern, Jerusalem, 283-291.

Snodgrass, A.M. 1971. *The Dark Age of Greece*. Edinburgh.

1974. Metal-work as Evidence for Immigration in the Late Bronze Age. In *Bronze Age Migrations in the Aegean. Archaeological and Linguistic Problems in Greek Prehistory*, eds. R.A. Crossland & A. Birchall, Park Ridge, 209-214.

1980a. Iron and early metallurgy in the Mediterranean. In *The Coming of the Age of Iron*, eds. T.A. Wertime and J.D. Muhly, New Haven, 335-374.

1980b. *Archaic Greece. The age of experiment*. London, Melbourne & Toronto.

1983. Cyprus and the beginnings of iron technology in the eastern Mediterranean. In *Early metallurgy in Cyprus, 4000-500 BC*, eds. J.D. Muhly, R. Maddin and V. Karageorghis, Nicosia, 285-294.

1987. The Early Iron Age of Greece. In *An Archaeology of Ancient Greece*, Berkeley, Los Angeles and London, 170-210.

1989. The Coming of the Age of Iron in Greece: Europe's Earliest Bronze/Iron Transition. In *The Bronze Age Iron Age Transition in Europe. Aspects of Continuity and Change in European societies 1200-500 BC*, (BAR -Int 483 (i)), eds. M.L. Stig Sørensen and R. Thomas, Oxford, 22-35.

1993. The rise of the polis: the archaeological evidence. In *The Ancient Greek City-State*, ed. M.H. Hansen, Copenhagen, 30-40.

Stein, G. & Rothman, M.S. eds. 1994. *Chiefdoms and Early States in the Near East: The Organizational Dynamics of Complexity*. Madison, Wisc.

Tallgren, A.M., 1916, Sveriges förbindelser med Ryssland under bronsåldern, *Finsk tidskrift*.

1937. *The Arctic Bronze Age in Europe*. (Eurasia Septentrionalis Antiqua (ESA) XI). Helsinki.

Thrane, H. 1993. From Mini to Maxi. Bronze Age Barrows from Funen as Illustration of Variation and Structure. In *Bronsålderns gravhögar. Rapport från ett symposium i Lund 15-16/11 1991*, ed. L. Larsson (Inst. of Archaeology. Report Series, 48), Lund, 79-92.

Vankilde, H. 1996. *From Stone to Bronze. The Metalwork of the Late Neolithic and Earliest Bronze Age in Denmark*. Aarhus.

Vanschoonwinkel, J. 1991. *L'Égée et la Méditerranée orientale à la fin du deuxième millénaire* (Archaeologia Transatlantica 10). Louvain-la-Neuve & Providence.

Varoufakis, G.J. 1983. The origin of Mycenaean and Geometric iron in the Greek Mainland and the Aegean islands. In *Early metallurgy in Cyprus, 4000-500 BC*, eds. J.D. Muhly, R. Maddin & V. Karageorghis, Nicosia, 315-322.

1989. Greece: An Important Metallurgical Centre of Iron in Antiquity. In *Archaeometallurgy of Iron. International Symposium of the Comité pour la sidérurgie ancienne de l'UISPP. Liblice, 5-9 October 1987*, ed. R. Pleiner, Prague, 279-286.

Vedel, E. 1886. *Bornholms oldtidsminder og oldsaker*. København.

Waldbaum, J.C. 1978. *From bronze to iron. The transition from the Bronze Age to the Iron Age in the Eastern Mediterranean* (SIMA 54). Göteborg.

1980. The First Archaeological Appearance of Iron and the Transition to the Iron Age. In *The Coming of the Age of Iron*, eds. T.A. Wertime and J.D. Muhly, New Haven, 69-98.

1983. Bimetallic Objects from the Eastern Mediterranean and the Question of the Dissemination of Iron. In *Early metallurgy in Cyprus, 4000-500 BC*, eds. J.D. Muhly, R. Maddin and V. Karageorghis, Nicosia, 325-347.

1989. Copper, Iron, Tin, Wood; The Start of the Iron Age in the Eastern Mediterranean. *Archaeomaterials* 3: 11-122.

Ward, W.A. & Sharp Joukowksy, M. eds. 1992. *The Crisis Years: the 12th Century BC: from beyond the Danube to the Tigris*. Dubuque.

Warren P. & Hankey, V.1989. *Aegean Bronze Age Chronology*. Bristol.

Wertime, T. 1973. The Beginnings of Metallurgy: A New Look. *Science* 182, 875-887.

& Muhly, J. eds.1980. *The Coming of the Age of Iron*. New Haven.

Whitley, J. 1991. Social diversity in Dark Age Greece. *BSA* 86: 341-365.

Eva Hjärthner-Holdar and Christina Risberg: The Innovation of Iron.

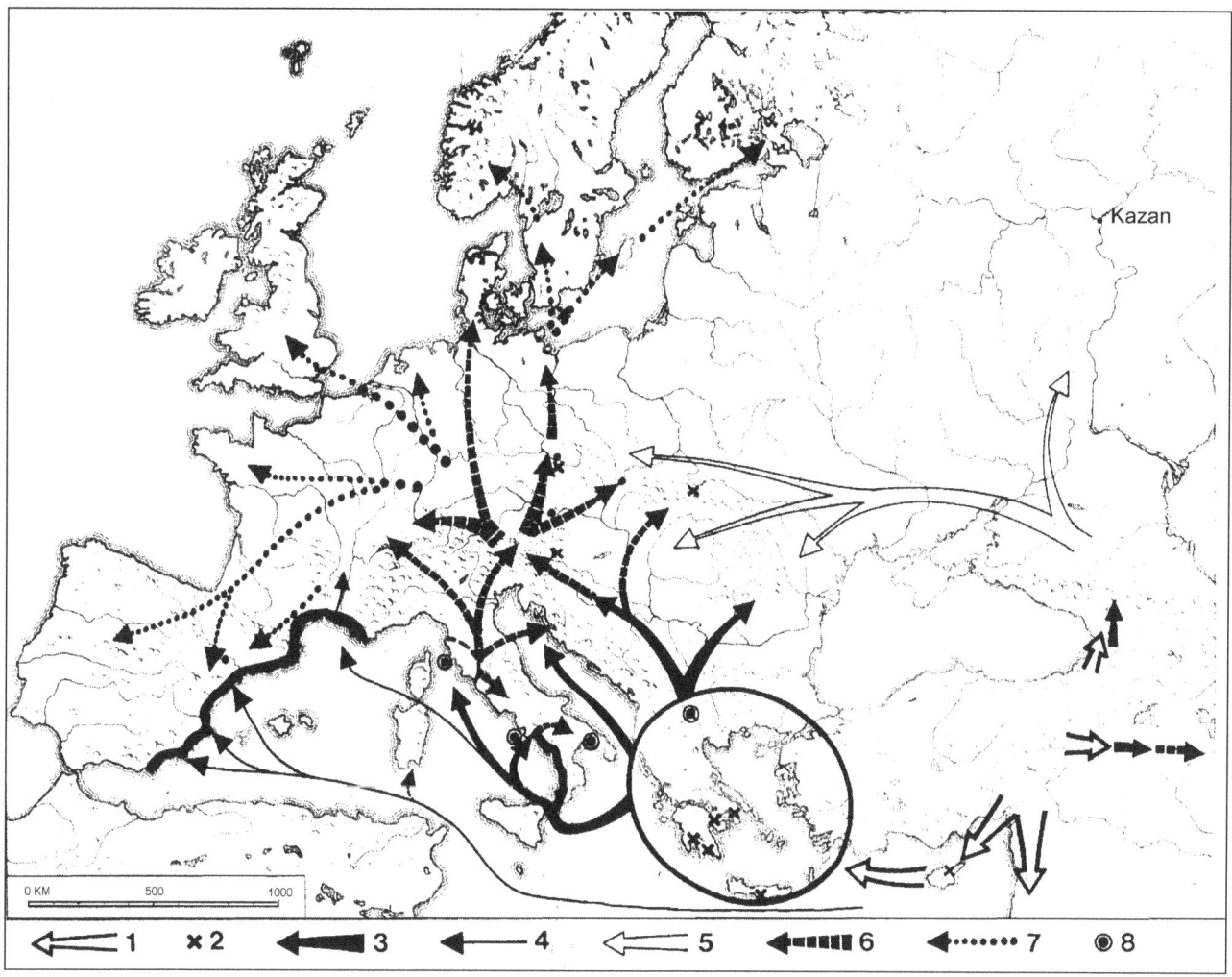

Fig.1. The spread of iron in Eurasia: 1) second half of the second millennium BC in Asia and Eastern Mediterranean 2) sporadic occurrence of iron objects. 3) the area of Greece with earliest finds and with primary directions of spreading 4) Phoenician influences 5) Cimmerian and Scythian influences 6) iron in Central Europe and Italy in the Late Bronze Age and beginning of the Iron Age 7) spread of iron in the North and West of Europe about 500 BC and 8) important early metallurgical activity. After R. Pleiner 1980: fig 11.2.

Cultural Interactions in Europe and the Eastern Mediterranean during the Bronze Age (3000-500 BC)

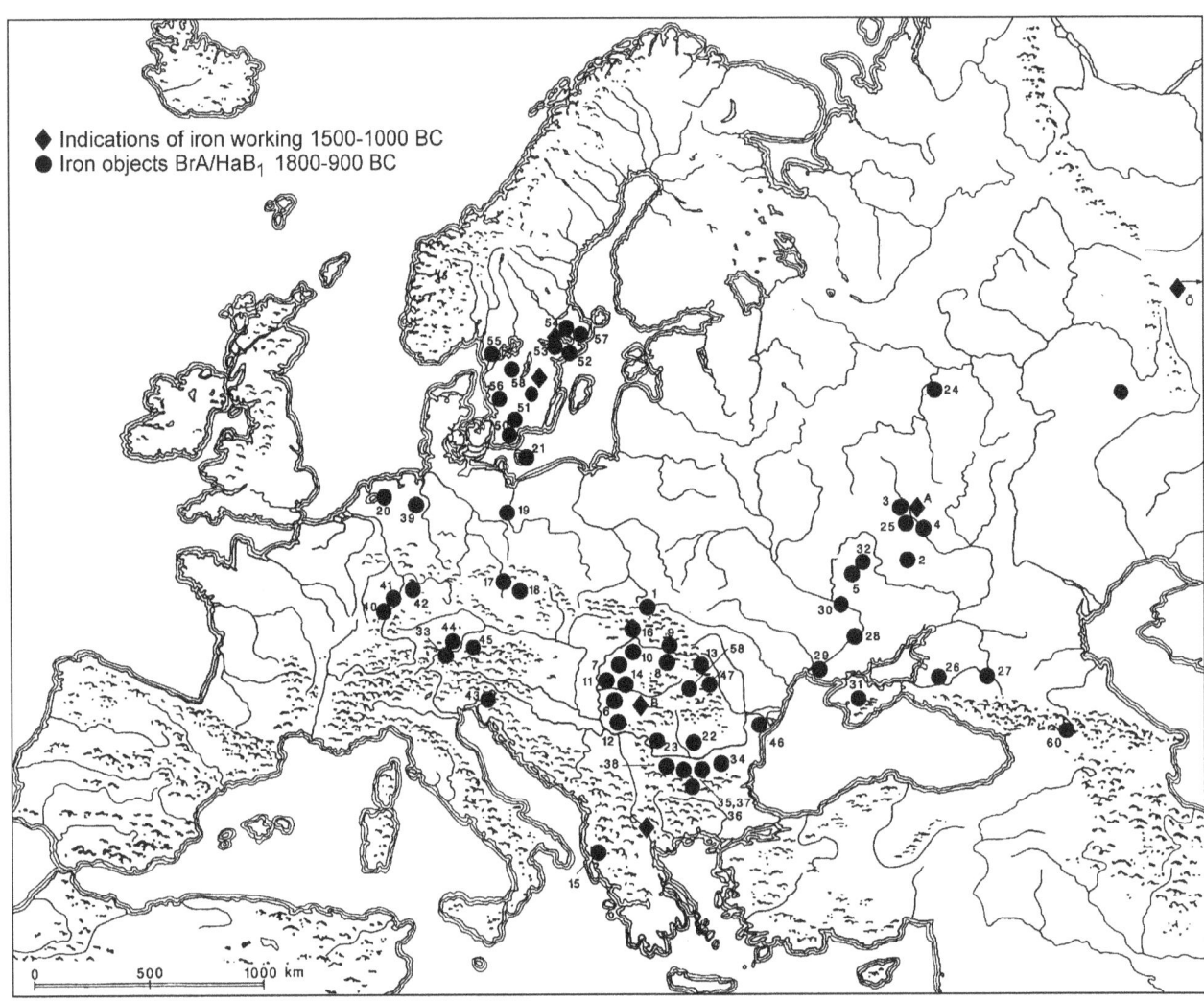

Fig.2. Early iron objects and iron production in Eurasia during the period 1800-900 BC. After Hjärthner-Holdar 1993, Fig. 5 with additions.

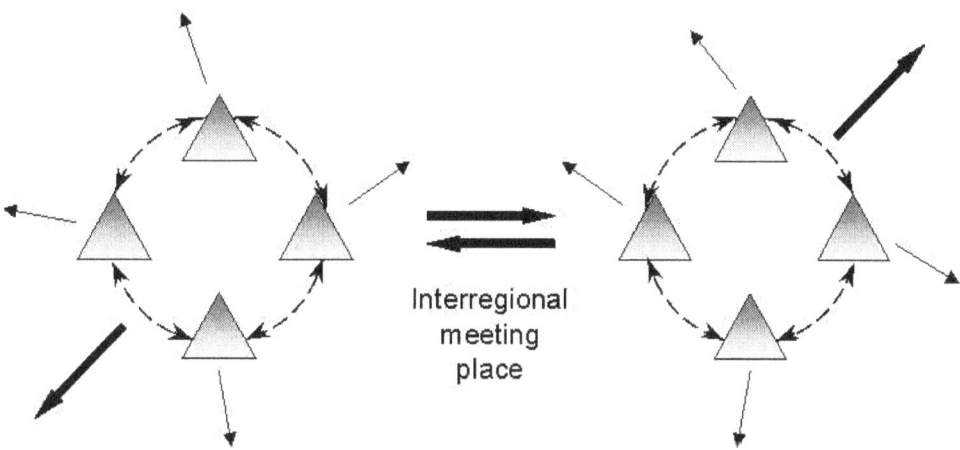

Fig. 3. Model of internal and external interactions in East and Central Sweden during period III-V of the Bronze Age.

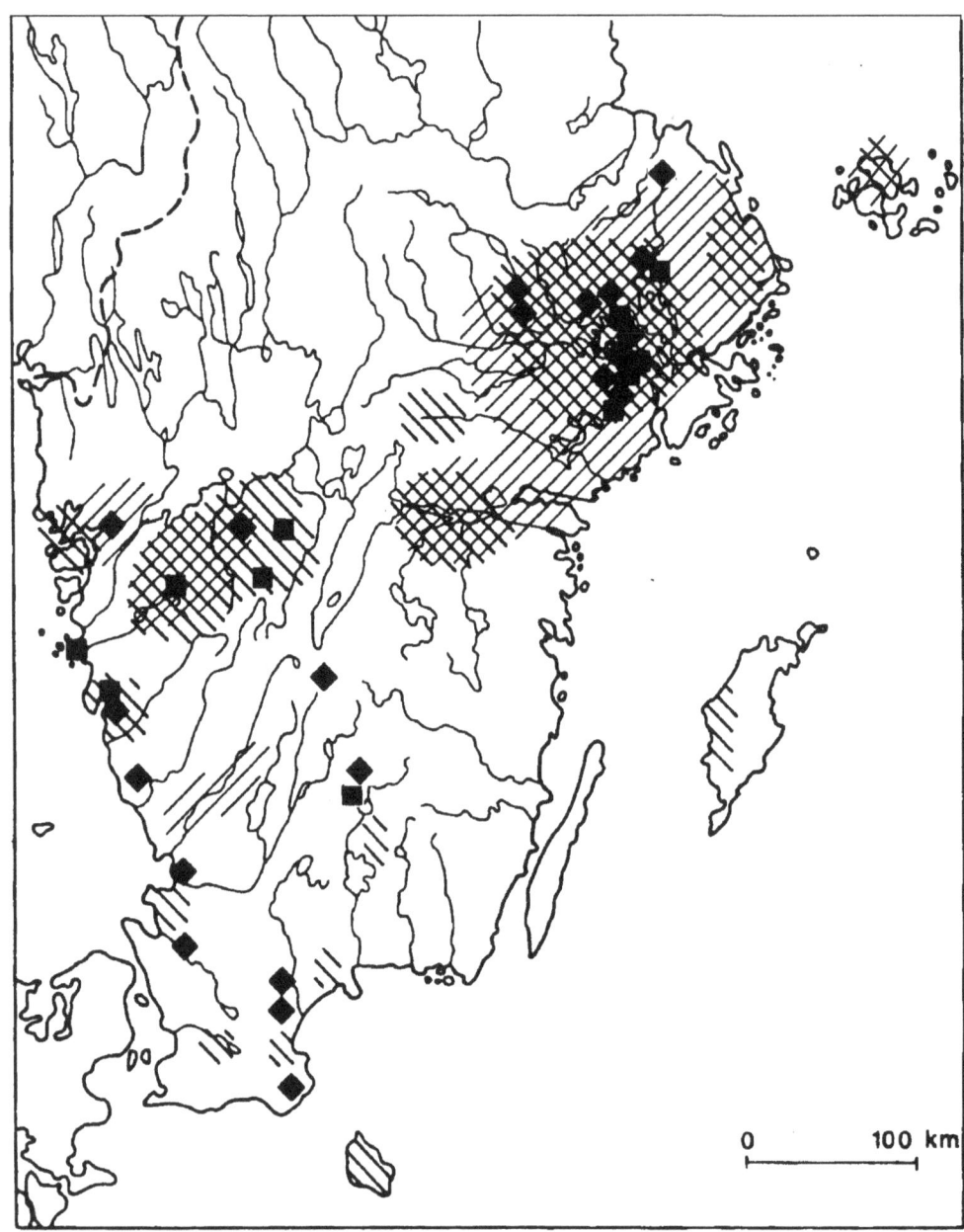

- ◆ Iron objects dated before period VI
- ■ Iron slags dated before period VI
- //// Striated ware
- ⧹⧹⧹⧹ Mälardalen celts (after Baudou 1960)

Fig.4. The distribution of striated ware, Mälardalen celts, iron objects from Montelius period III-V (1300-700 BC) and iron production *before* period Montelius period VI of the Bronze Age (before 7th BC).

Fig.5. Iron objects in the Aegean, c. 1100–900 BC. After Snodgrass 1980a.

Fig.6. Example of striated ware from a cemetery in Uppland. (Photo E. Hjärthner-Holdar).

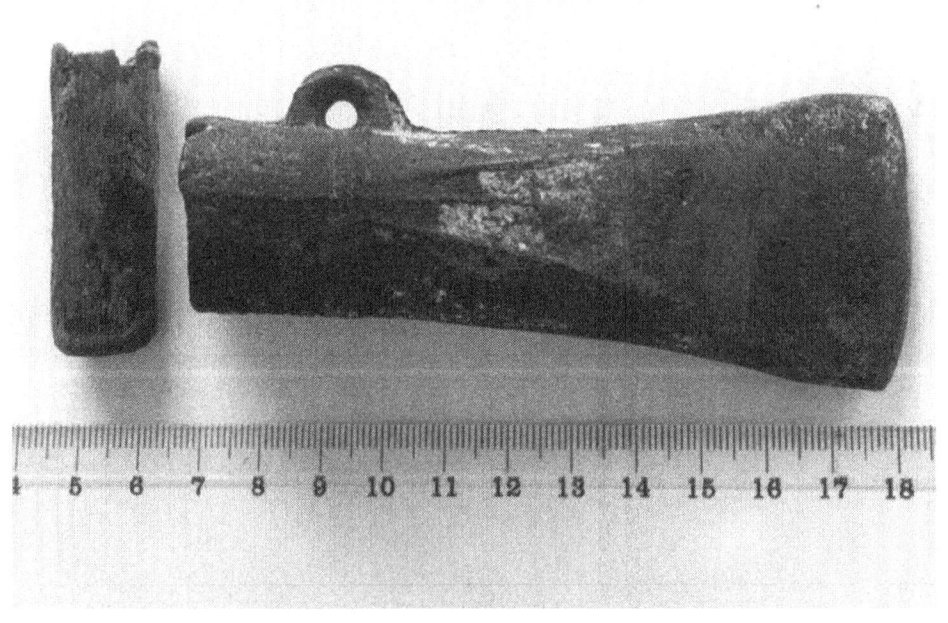

Fig.7. A Mälardalen celt found in Uppland. (Photo P. Kresten, GAL).

Diffusion, Dissemination and Interaction
The contradictions of past realities or of present perspectives

Luiz Oosterbeek

The debates on cultural change, in the last decade of the XXth Century, seem to fall in the Babel trap: many arguments in different languages, producing a crossing of divergent approaches. Diffusion and evolutionist perspectives interbreed, and a large number of "possibilities" arise, under the scope of "complexification". The archaeological record seems to provide help for almost all sorts of perspectives, throughing more and more scholars into eclectic theories. Yet, the contradictions of the archaeological record may, in fact, reflect biased approaches to it.

Between stability and change, Prehistoric studies, although devoting a large attention to spatial studies, focus on change, and on the modalities of change, identifying four main types:

- deviation, i.e. change caused by a non predictable separation from the rule (social fission may be interpreted as a deviation from the social complexification process);
- evolution, i.e. progressive change dominated by assimilation procedures (the neolitization is currently interpreted as such);
- revolution, i.e. dramatic change, dominated by accommodation procedures, be them derived from external (e.g. the introduction of metallurgy in Iberia) or internal factors (the warfare associated to the "barbarian Europe");
- mutation, i.e. change that leads to a final result with limited relations with its origin (this being the case of the emergence of kingdoms).

This characteristic of prehistoric studies is the opposite of technological ones that focus on spatial issues, on the relations and boundaries between objects. But, clearly, the space as seen from the perspective of technology is not the cultural space, socially built, that concerns us.

It is in this context that many authors look for an "escape", trying to promote an eclectic approach, simultaneously promoting the "scientific" status of Humanistic studies (inheritance of neo-positivist new archaeology) and questioning the objectivity of knowledge (post-processual influence); all in all refusing the unity of knowledge.

In our opinion, scientific analysis remains useful, but it is no longer the crucial part of the knowledge process (as it has been for modernity); transdiciplinarity, synthesis, and *praxis,* have taken its place.

Because the knowledge process is one, theory and method cannot be isolated from each other. Yet, method has the advantage, over theory, to have escaped, to a large extent, to the sterile debates of the XXth Century. This consensus on methodological issues led many scholars to identify in it an illusive unity, or complementarity of different theoretical approaches, and hence tried to conciliate these.

Method is the instrument of the knowledge. Despite the epistemological crisis of the last hundred years, methodology kept on improving, based on the rational system previously built. Because the various theories later developed, from historico-culturalism to functionalism, from the new archaeology to post-processualism, all remained in the field of analysis, and were impotent to comply with the needs stated above, they were, also, unable to develop their own methods. Because, in any case, they required some kind of methodology, they kept on using the dialectic rationalist method, or parts of it, thus generating the contemporary transversality of the method.

Knowledge is a social process, and depends upon the cognitive relation (that defines its "objectivity") and language (the knowledge interface), and both are misleading. The nature of knowledge refuses the separation between theory and practice; it builds from action, as a *praxis*, and gets its legitimacy from the *polis*, the society. In this sense, knowledge is, always, political.

Present perspectives, the only perspectives that may be conceptualised by contemporary societies, hence, guide the past realities. This has nothing to do with subjectiveness, it is the nature of objective social knowledge, but it is, obviously, different from objectivity in physics or geometry. In the case of prehistoric studies, including palaeoenvironment related ones; the subject of study is separated from us in time, whereas in the so-called *natural sciences* it is mainly separated in space. The more historical the distance is between us and our topic of study, the greater is the social impact on the reading of the record.

The transition to the Bronze Age in Iberia is often read as the emergence of complex chiefdoms and, ultimately, of the State. It is also understood as the crossing of diffusion mechanisms, associated to the "barbarian" Europe, recently re-baptised as "golden age". These mechanisms are related to the Phoenicians and the Atlantic Bronze Age, the arguments being often restricted to the discussion on the relevance of indigenous contributions.

More recently, the idea of contact, or encounter, as tried to replace that of conquest and diffusion. This idea probably accounts for a better understanding of the interactions between endogenous and exogenous contributions.

In order to assess the mechanisms of spread, or convergence, of new social, economic and technological realities, one must first define the territories considered. In fact, some concepts, like diffusion, will only have a meaning if corresponding to processes of linkage between different territories (these being socially defined).

It is our view that most of Europe became, in the process of the agro-pastoral spread, a single territory, although decomposable in smaller regional units. This means that, for each single community, the endogenous interactions were to be established, without considering diffusion (abrupt spread) or even dissemination (persuasive spread) as major mechanisms. In such a context, interaction should be the dominant mechanism, even if interaction between unequal societies does not exclude domination and imposition processes. But these have to be read as internal to the logical evolution of the society, and not as a clash with the outer world.

The second millennium is dominated by a certain number of changing trends:

- a decrease in importance of the hillforts, and an increase in the number and variety of settlements, often of small dimensions (a phenomena that has been understood by some as sign of social fission);
- a decrease in the visibility of funerary monuments, with the emergence of rock-cut tombs, false corbelled chambers and small cists, indicating a decrease in the investment of labour in them;
- a greater diversity in the funerary solutions, including a greater differentiation of the votive items and the increase of individual burials;
- the slow but steady increase of metallic prestige items (copper, bronze) in burials and ceremonial precincts, including the so-called "deposits";
- the occurrence of stelae, indicating a new management of the landscape and a new religious pantheon, also suggested by the new rock-art galician-portuguese cycle, in a context where even the Mediterranean "sacred mountain" could be present (at "Cabeço da Mina").

All in all, the transition to the Bronze Age may be characterised by less "public" works, more attention to the individuals (or certain individuals), greater diversity and a new religion. Should we read these as a result of external influences?

The archaeological record seems to point in contradictory directions: it indicates a shift, with links to the Mediterranean and Atlantic contexts, but it also suggests continuity in the stratigraphies, rarity to absence of exogenous artifacts, etc.

Yet, if one considers the Portuguese territory as part of a West-Southern cultural complex, all these changes become a result of the internal dynamics of the chalcolithic chiefdoms, in a process that, tendentially, is leading to the state formation (to be achieved in Central and Eastern Europe first).

Hence, the question should be no longer "where from?" (the answer being: "within"!), nor "how" (dissemination, diffusion and interaction being all acceptable processes within the European space, thus their detailed identification becoming matter for regional and local studies) but "why"?

No economic or demographic processes may account for the shift (they are descriptive, but not explanatory), and no external invasions either. The "why" must be sought, again, "within", i.e., in the social contradictions generated throughout the implementation of agro-pastoralism. The new evidences, ideological rather than economic in a first stage, stand for the consolidation of elite's, that will use new symbols, including exotic items, for this purpose.

The changes recorded in the second millennium, and the apparent contradictions mentioned above, may in fact be read as a social and political process, with conflicting possibilities: the clear imposition of a new elite of individuals (and no longer only of lineages) or the continuation of the previous ranking system. We do not share the opinion that the second possibility, through a mechanism of social fission, might have had any significant impact in the Portuguese territory. On the contrary, we think that all major evidence, mentioned above, indicate that the shift took place, with the decay of the still "collectivist" solutions (large hillforts of megaliths) to the profit of the contexts for the benefit of individuals (less costly in labour, but more effective for the elite).

The indicators of an increasing exchange of prestige items (polished stone, metals, decorative patters) are not to be explained by any major displacements of population (invasions or migrations), but by the continuation of a lasting practice of travelling, already present from the upper Palaeolithic, and undoubtedly reinforced in the context of this social process.

What is, then, the sense of this shift? In our opinion, it must be read as the climax of the agro-pastoralist model, characterised by the domestication of the land, the humanisation (privatisation!) of the landscapes (with the corresponding decrease of mobility), and as a name: the emergence of the State, in its essential version (men in arms, protecting themselves, their way of managing the society, and their privileges).

References

Balmuth, Miriam S., Antonio Gilman, Lourdes Prados-Torreira (s.d.), *Encounters and Transformations. The archaeology of Iberia in Transition*, Monographs in Mediterranean Archaeology 7, Sheffield Academic Press

Jorge, Susana O. 1999. *Domesticar a Terra. As primeiras comunidades agrárias em território português*, Lisboa, Ed. Gradiva

Larsson, Thomas B. 1999. The transmission of an élite ideology – Europe and the Near East in the second millennium BC, IN: J. Goldhahn (ed.), *Rock Art as social Representation. Papers from a session held at the European Association of Archaeologists Fourth Annual Meeting in Göteborg 1998*, Oxford, BAR International Series # 794

Lillios, Katina 1991. *Competition to Fission: the Copper to Bronze Age transition in he lowlands of west central Portugal (3000-1000 B.C.)*, Yale University, PhD dissertation

Oosterbeek, Luiz 1997. War in the Chalcolithic? The meaning of western Mediterranean hillforts. In: J.Carman (ed.) *Material Harm: Archaeological Studies of War and Violence*, Glasgow, Cruithne Press, 116-132

Oosterbeek, Luiz 1997. Echoes from the East: late prehistory of the North Ribatejo, Tomar, CEIPHAR, "Arkeos" vol.2

Cultural Interactions in Europe and the Eastern Mediterranean during the Bronze Age (3000-500 BC)

Long-distance cultural interaction in megalithic Europe: Carrowmore and the Irish megalithic tradition in a western European and Mediterranean context

Göran Burenhult

Apparent similarities in the megalithic world of symbols in Western Europe have been subject to intense debate during much of the 20th century, both regarding art and tomb morphology. At the same time, distinctive regional features and assemblages of symbols can easily be defined in most areas. The possible existence of long distance contact networks, from the Iberian Peninsula in the South to western Norway in the north, has been highlighted by several scholars. What is the evidence for this, and how can it be used to explain widely spread similarities within the contemporary megalithic traditions?

An equivalent direct interaction including the Mediterranean world as a model for explanation has, however, not been subject to a more detailed analysis in recent times. This paper will raise the question on possible direct relations between the contemporary Mediterranean societies and their symbolic world and the western European megalith-building societies during the peak of the megalithic tradition, c. 3500-3000 B.C. Also, if such close regular connections did exist, how can they be physically explained, and in what ways did they affect the Neolithic societies along the Atlantic coasts? New archaeological, ethno-archaeological and ethno-historical data from the Pacific area regarding the appearance and evolution of megalithic traditions may produce possible food for thought to the western European and Mediterranean cases.

The western European networks

In 1975, as a graduate student, I had the honour of visiting the ongoing excavations at Newgrange in the Boyne Valley in Ireland under the guidance of the excavator, the Late Professor Michael J. O'Kelly. After a long and interesting tour and deep discussions regarding the famous artwork, Professor O'Kelly took me to the back of the monument, and showed me kerbstone no. 52. This particular kerbstone has a deep, vertical groove, which divides the stone in two halves. The artwork on one side of the groove is distinctly different to that of the other (fig. 1a). Professor O'Kelly revealed to me his own interpretation of this. The carvings on the left side of the groove show very typical examples of Irish passage tomb art: spirals and rhombic patterns (fig. 1b). The right-hand side of the kerbstone, however, shows boxed U-shaped patterns, which have their closest counterparts in the famous passage tomb of Gavrinis in Brittany, France (fig. 1c). I believe, he said, that at this stage, during the megalithic peak, about 3200 B.C., the priests, or divine chiefs, of megalithic western Europe were in regular and close contact with each other, and maybe also travelled frequently, visiting each others' ceremonies at regular intervals. Professor O'Kellys' conclusion was that the patterns on kerbstone 52 may well represent the regional symbolic worlds of the Boyne Valley and Brittany, but also symbolises the common megalithic cult in western Europe.

A series of different approaches to the problem of long-distance Neolithic networks in western Europe have been presented during the 20th century, with explanations from pure diffusion to intense trade, exchange systems and networks. Early in the century, Oscar Montelius (1905) made an attempt to link the Scandinavian cup mark symbols to similar figures in the west European megalithic context. Also, P.V. Glob (1969:163-168) strongly stressed the similarities within the Middle Neolithic west European symbolic world, with its schematic signs and the overall connection to the mother Goddess, both within the Funnel Neck Beaker culture and later within the Beaker/Battle Axe culture complexes. The well documented, somewhat later evidence of long-distance contacts between northern Europe and Britain and Ireland with the exchange of luxury items of gold, copper and bronze, is important in this context (Burenhult 1999:68-69).

Based on certain motifs in the western Norwegian rock art, Eva and Per Fett (1980) suggested another interaction zone between Scandinavia and Western Europe, and pointed out close similarities between figures in Ausevik, Gavrinis and the Boyne Valley (fig. 1). I have elsewhere stressed that the rich variety of motifs on the south Scandinavian Funnel Neck Beaker megalithic pottery is identical to the ones that appear as carvings on megalithic tombs in Western Europe, and suggested that the same symbols were adopted to different regional traditions and ceremonies in connection with the burials (Burenhult 1980b: 104, 106-107, 121, 133-134, 1999:68-71). Elizabeth Shee Twohig (1981) drew attention to the fact that only a minority of the decorative traits are shared between the regions in which art occurs, and that Ireland's closest links are with Brittany, rather than Iberia (1981:136-40).

The existence of a series of inter-regional links between Ireland and other areas of Western Europe in the fourth millennium BC has been suggested by Richard Bradley and Robert Chapman (1984). These contacts, as shown in the appearance of similar motifs, seem to belong to a developed stage in the megalithic sequence (1984:352), and its only towards the culmination of this that explicit links between various regions can be traced. As the megalithic societies grew in complexity, access to exotic objects, and ritual knowledge may have become of increasing importance (1984:354). Bradley has recently (1997) further developed these suggestions for western and south-western Europe, convincingly showing possible interaction zones during the Neolithic and Bronze Age between Britain, Ireland, France, Galicia and Portugal, where especially the long-distance contacts in Atlantic Europe are highlighted in a comparison of Galician and Scottish rock art (1997:21-26, 44, 208-216).

However, not only art, pottery and tomb morphology point to a common megalithic world of symbols in western Europe. Also certain ceremonial artefacts show great similarities in several regions, indicating close contacts and a common ritual symbolism. Similarities regarding carved bone work from the Boyne Valley tombs and Iberian counterparts have been highlighted by George Eogan (1979). Another example is the famous pointed, extraordinary sandstone, decorated half-cylinder-shaped object from the Knowth passage tomb in the Boyne Valley, Ireland (fig. 2d). Its counterparts appear in Portuguese megalithic tombs, especially in the Estremadura district, where a series of, mostly decorated, half-cylinders made of sandstone have been found (fig. 2a-c and 3).

Can we exclude frequent, direct contacts with the Mediterranean area in this context in the second half of the fourth millennium BC, and, if not, are there any symbolic elements in the contemporary societies which indicate such contacts? How can we physically explain the extent of the total, inter-regional network – and where are the geographical limits? First, however, we have to consider the development of the megalithic tradition in western Europe as such, by looking at new data from Irish megalithic tombs.

Carrowmore and the Irish passage tomb tradition

There is today general agreement that the evolution of megalithic structures in Atlantic Europe can be explained as a development from simple to more complex constructions. In Ireland, this is particularly obvious regarding the passage tomb tradition and its magnificent cemeteries. Both size and complexity increased over time, reaching a peak with the mega-monuments of the Boyne Valley for example, that is that small and simple monuments are early, and the large and complex monuments belong to a late phase (Burenhult 1980a:115, 1999:63; O'Kelly 1981:182; Sheridan 1985/6; Cooney & Grogan 1994:57; Waddell 1998:77). Also, the appearance of artwork can be shown to belong to this later phase. There is a growing awareness that this development took place in landscapes that were significant long before larger tombs were built in them, as shown e.g. within the Irish passage tomb tradition (Eogan 1986; Bergh 1995:119-121; Cooney 2000:163-173). New data from the Carrowmore megalithic cemetery strongly supports this development.

The layout and structure of the Carrowmore cemetery is clearly that of an arranged ritual landscape, where the tombs have been placed in an oval shape around an area where no tombs, with the exception of the major monument at Carrowmore, Tomb No. 51 (*Listoghil*), were erected (Bergh 1995:119-121; Cooney 1990:750; 2000:163-164). There is a clear tendency that the tomb entrances, in eight out of the ten cases where this can be established, are facing towards the central part of the cemetery, that is the tombs on the western side of the cemetery are facing eastwards, while the tombs on the eastern side are facing westwards (Bergh 1995:126). The direction of the entrances of two of the northernmost tombs in the cemetery oval falls completely out of this picture, but this still suggests, however, that the layout must have been deliberately planned already when the very first tombs were erected at Carrowmore.

In the late 70's, a series of radiocarbon dates from Tomb Nos 4, 7 and 27 placed the initial phase of the Carrowmore cemetery in the fifth and early fourth millennia BC. Inevitably, the excavation results and the following interpretations gave rise to an intense debate and were subject to severe criticism, partly because the earliest dates would imply a Mesolithic rather than Neolithic subsistence-settlement system for the megalith-building society (Burenhult 1980a, 1984:133-140; Caulfield 1983:206-213; ApSimon 1986). To some extent, controversy still surrounds the earliest dates from the first excavation campaign at Carrowmore (Grogan 1991; Cooney & Grogan 1994; Bergh 1995:102-104; Thorpe 1996:102; Waddell 1998; Cooney 2000:223). The recent investigations of the Swedish Archaeological Excavations at Carrowmore (1994-1998) have involved the excavation of six previously unexcavated tombs within the cemetery, Tombs Nos 1, 13, 19, 51, 55A and 56. Also, an additional excavation of a third quadrant of Tomb No. 4, two quadrants of which were excavated in 1979, was undertaken in 1994.

Radiocarbon evidence from the new excavation campaign strongly supports the results from the 70's and early 1980's. The oldest dates so far available from the Carrowmore megalithic cemetery comes from Tomb No. 4. The primary construction was seemingly built about 5000 BC, two samples from the foundations to the stones in the cist have been dated to c. 5400 BC and 4800 respectively. During the second phase, a small passage and an inner stone circle was added. Three radiocarbon samples, dated to c. 4350 BC, 4200 BC, and 3800 BC respectively, are found in this context, and can be connected to this phase of use. The third and final phase of the monument has been dated to about 3000 BC, when a second inner stone circle was added, in which two secondary stone cists were built (fig. 4) (Burenhult 2001, and *in preparation*; Burenhult & Possnert *in preparation*).

Additional samples which have produced radiocarbon dates from the fifth millennium BC have been found in Tomb No. 1 (c. 4350 BC), and Tomb No. 7 (c. 4200 BC) (fig. 3). Between 4000 and 3500 BC, also Tomb No. 19 (c. 3950 BC), Tomb No. 27 (c. 3900 BC), Tomb No. and Tomb No. 55A (c. 3800 BC), were in use. At the end of this period, the first dates from Tomb No. 51 appear (c. 3650 BC).

The positioning in the centre of the cemetery, and the original features of Tomb No. 51 gives the monument a significant, focal role in the Carrowmore Megalithic Cemetery context. The size of the site, with a diameter of 32 metres, as well as the existence of the remains of a cairn, marks a sharp difference between Tomb No. 51 and all other preserved monuments in the cemetery. Also, the chamber itself, constructed as a rectangular cist or chamber, covered with a flat, limestone roof-slab, makes the monument unique among the Carrowmore tombs. Moreover, in 1993, circular carvings were found on the front side of the roof-slab, the first appearance of megalithic art at Carrowmore (Currán-Mulligan 1994:14).

Tomb No. 51 was partially excavated by the Swedish team in 1996-98. The complete central chamber area, as well as three test trenches through the cairn, were investigated. Also, the well preserved boulder circle, built of more than a hundred stones, was exposed. An evaluation of the results, based on excavation data and radiocarbon dates available today, suggests the following course of construction and use of Tomb No. 51.

Before the erection of the monument, the contemporary grass sod and topsoil was completely removed. A layer of light brown sterile moraine seems then to have been evenly spread out over the area, approximately 25 cm thick. During this procedure, ritual activities took place, involving extensive fires, and heavily burnt areas have been documented, also embedded in this layer, including finds of artefacts. The central chamber was erected in this context, and the orthostats were placed upon, or partly in, this layer.

A long series of radiocarbon dates (9 dated samples) indicate that these activities took place some time between 3650 and 3450 BC. Also, a number of pits were dug down into the layer during these activities, and in one of them, a large concentration of charcoal was placed. Radiocarbon dates from these pits confirm that all these activities were more or less contemporary, centering around 3550 BC.

It is likely that the boulder circle was created in the same context. As the boulders in the circle are placed directly upon the brown layer, it cannot have been built before the construction of the layer itself. At some stage after the completion of the boulder circle, two cremations containing several humans were deposited in the circle behind the southern and the western kerbstones respectively. The final building stage involved the construction of the cairn itself. It is not possible to determine the time-span between the erection of the central chamber and the final building of the cairn. However, the date at c. 3500 BC from a piece of a human skull shows that inhumations took place within the determined initial building period.

Consequently, all available evidence suggests that the major monument at Carrowmore, Tomb No. 51, was built and used towards the very end of the Carrowmore megalithic sequence, and so far only Tomb No. 56 has produced possible later construction dates (fig. 4). However, the site of Tomb No. 51 as such clearly must have had a focal significance to the tomb builders long before that. There are possible indications that an earlier monument on the site pre-dates Tomb No. 51. Three large boulders, that do not seemingly form any constructional part of the tomb, were found beside the central chamber, possibly the remains of a destroyed megalithic construction. Furthermore, a massive stone-packing was found on the southern side of the monument, just outside the boulder circle, possibly the remains of a destroyed satellite monument. A radiocarbon sample from this area, dated to c. 4100 BC, may support this interpretation.

During the second excavation campaign at Carrowmore, another megalithic monument in the Knocknarea peninsula was excavated by the Swedish team, a court tomb at Primrose Grange, situated about two kilometres southwest of Carrowmore. The aim of the excavation was to study the chronological relationship between different tomb types in the region. Also, possible differences in burial practices and artefact assemblages could be of vital importance to the interpretation of social and ritual systems within the Stone Age societies in the Knocknarea peninsula.

The excavation of the Primrose Grange court tomb revealed that this monument was in use during the same period as the Carrowmore tombs, although fundamental differences in tomb morphology, burial practices and grave-goods could be documented. Radiocarbon samples from the central chamber have provided dates from between c. 4300 and 3000 BC. The burials found in the Primrose Grange tomb are almost all inhumations, and very few cremated bones have been found. At Carrowmore, only in Tomb No. 51 have inhumations been found. Also, the artefacts associated with the burials are very different. The typical Carrowmore assemblage consists of mushroom-headed antler pins and stone/clay-balls, artefacts that have not been found at Primrose Grange. Instead, extraordinary pieces of chert artefacts were found, mainly leaf-shaped or pointed arrow-heads.

It is conceivable that the evolution of "central monuments" in focal places reflects far-reaching social change within the megalithic societies in western Europe in the mid-fourth millennium BC. Also, the contemporary use of different "types" of tombs and different assemblages of artefacts, may indicate that they should be interpreted as symbols of communal position, group or clan affiliation, or heredity rank, in the local society (e.g. Darvill 1979; Sheridan 1985/86; Cooney & Grogan 1994; Burenhult 1999). It has been suggested that this evolution was enforced by intense long-distance contacts between elites in western Europe, which had the rights to build and use these monuments, and carved motifs, and a specific set of artefacts. Maybe the more complex, contemporary societies in the Mediterranean area actively produced currents of ideas in this process?

Mediterranean contacts? Malta and the British Isles

During the peak of the megalithic tradition in western Europe, c. 3500-3000 BC, the western Mediterranean societies in many places experienced a remarkable social change, reflected in the development of complex megalithic structures, e.g the Millarian sites in southeast Spain (fig. 3). Some of the tombs have corbelled vaults, and many are decorated inside. The find material suggests long-distance exchange, among other things African ivory and ostrich shell. The largest tombs, containing the largest quantities of exotic goods, seem to act as foci for the rest, and it has been suggested that these nucleated cemeteries reflect established social ranking (Savory 1968; Chapman 1981; Champion *et al* 1984:148). Also, the existence of fortification reflects social differentiation.

Another, even more striking example of this social change, as reflected in monumental architecture, is found on the island of Malta. Between 4000 and 3000 BC, at least twelve major temple complexes were erected, built in several phases over a long period of time. They all seem to be distributed in pairs or clusters, and are characterized by a series of absidal courts or chambers, arranged on either side of a central corridor opening from a monumental facade. Other characteristics are altar-like constructions, niches and port-holes (Evans 1959, 1971; Trump 1966, 1972; Renfrew 1973; Müller-Karpe 1974; Burenhult 1981:75-121; Champion et al 1984:149; Trump, Bonanno, Gouder, Malone & Stoddart 1993:100-101). The irregular shape of the temples is identical to the shape of the rock-cut tombs, which were used for burials, both before the building of the first monuments, and during the temple phase of the island. It is obvious, that the megalithic architects copied the final resting rooms for the dead in creating the magnificent temples above ground. Maybe this also gives us an idea of the rituals performed in the monuments, which is regarded to be based on ancestral cult.

In conclusion, it seems as if the contemporary societies in the western Mediterranean and in Atlantic Europe during the fourth millennium BC developed much of the same traditions regarding monumental architecture and in the layout of ceremonial sites. Although regional peculiarities, in most cases, are very apparent, a series of remarkable structural and symbolic similarities can be found in Ireland and Britain. The passage tombs in Ireland with their cruciform chambers show architectural traits, which can be discussed in a Maltese context; monumental entrances and passages, absidal chambers and altar-like constructions (fig. 5).

But there are also similarities in distinct features in the artwork, which have to be considered. The famous carved entrance-stone in the kerbstone circle at Newgrange in the Boyne Valley bear close resemblance to some of the altar-stones at the Tarxien temple on Malta, dominated by their carved spirals (fig. 6). Another distinct trait at Newgrange, which has its counterparts in several of the Maltese temples, is the peculiar surface pecking on a large number of the monoliths. This often total coverage of visible parts of the surface has sometimes been called *horror vacuii*, that is, for ritual or magic reasons, a fear of leaving exposed, natural surfaces of the stones visible. The idea is the same, although the technique differs, probably due to different rocks available. While the hard surface of the, mostly granite/gneiss, boulders at Newgrange has been completely dressed by pecking, the surface coverage in the Maltese temples consists of closely placed, drilled holes in the soft limestone boulders (fig. 7).

But not only the Irish passage tomb tradition show similarities with Maltese temples regarding constructional and symbolic features. Another extraordinary megalithic region in Western Europe, the island of Orkney in Scotland, shows unique peculiarities, which may not easily be discarded as coincidental. Impressive megalithic tombs, as Maes Howe, and gigantic stone henges, as the Ring of Brogar, indicate a complex ceremonial and ritual world on the island about 3000 BC, that is during the peak of the Maltese temple phase. In Bay of Skaill, the neolithic village of Skara Brae was in use between c. 3100 and 2500 BC. The extraordinary stone built houses, built into an older kitchen midden, are commonly regarded as belonging to a population of fishermen, although the remarkable interior, showing stone-built dressers, hearths, tables, cupboards and niches, have occasionally raised questions on a more ritual function of the site (Clarke & Maguire 1989).

The irregular layout of the Skara Brae houses and their interlinking passages, dug out in the midden, is very similar to the shape of the Maltese rock-cut tombs, and thereby also to the temples themselves (fig. 8 a-b). Also, the complex and symmetrically built stone furnishing in the Skara Brae houses bear close resemblance to the apses, niches and altars in the interior of the Maltese temples (fig. 8 c-d). This also applies to the hearts, "beds" and other stone-lined structures on the floors (fig. 7 c and f). Furthermore, the patterns on potsherds found at Skara Brae are identical to the carvings at Tarxien on Malta (fig. 8 e-f).

An attempt to, more in detail, explain all these seemingly close correspondences in the structural and symbolic, contemporary worlds in some regions of the western Mediterranean and megalithic western Europe would fall far outside the aim of this paper. Far-reaching, regional and inter-regional studies, taking into account all aspects of the archaeological and osteological record from the societies in question, will be necessary if we archaeologically are to support the idea of direct, long-distance contacts and influences. Instead, the main aim here is to discuss the physical possibilities for such contacts, as revealed from ethno-historical records on seafaring in the Pacific region.

The Pacific example

The conquest of the Pacfic Ocean surely is one of the major ventures in the history of humankind. During a period of more than 30 000 years, the isolated islands in a water space covering one third of the Earth were settled by skilled seafarers in open, outrigged canoes, challenging open water stretches often exceeding the distance between, say, Dublin and Rio de Janeiro, a distance equivalent to the one between New Caledonia and Easter Island, 9600 kilometres. This, of course, demanded not only advanced craftmanship and sailing skill, but also a deep knowledge of navigation, built on currents, winds and astronomical observations.

Island of Melanesia was settled from about 32 000 BC (Matenkupkum, New Ireland; Kilu, Buka about 27 000 BC) (Gosden 1993:77; White 1993:65-66). The earliest human occupation of Fiji took place about 1500 BC, Tonga and Samoa about 1100 BC. Eastern Polynesia saw the first voyagers after about AD 500, Hawaii c. AD 500, the Societies c. AD 600 and, Easter Island about AD 800. (Lewis 1972; Finney 1977; Irwin 1980; Bellwood 1989; Irwin 1990; Irwin, Bickler & Quirke 1990; Gosden 1991, 1992; Green 1993; Anderson 1994; Martinsson-Wallin 1998; Spriggs 1999). Between 3500 and 500 years ago, in a purely stone age context, the Polynesian sailors regularly covered distances of thousands of kilometers; the open water distance between, say, New Zealand and Tahiti is about 4800 kilometres, between Tahiti and Hawaíi about 4200 kilomctrcs.

These regular, long-distance voyages were evidently not the result of coincidential mis-navigations or accidents - or even less foolhardy undertakings. It is obvious, ... "that the voyagers were concerned for their safety, that their actions were deliberate, and that they did not have a mistaken view of their ocean world" (Irwin, Bickler & Quirke 1990:50). All available evidence seems to show that these initial landnams in Polynesia were the result of an expansion of people from the west towards the east: linguistic, DNA and material culture. However, at some stage, contacts with South America obviously were established, as shown by the appearance of the sweet potato and the white flower bottle gourd in the Pacific area, both plants endemic to the Americas (Martinsson-Wallin 1994; Skjølsvold 1994; Green 1998, 2000; Weisler 1998b).

During the final phase of this period, between AD 1100 and AD 1600, megalithic traditions emerged and developed over most of the Pacific area, and some of these regions gradually became important central places, displaying monumental architectural features related to strong elites in powerful chiefdoms, as e.g., Raiatea in the Societies, Pu'uhonua o Honauano on the big island of Hawaíi, or Nan Madol on Phonpei in Micronesia (fig. 9). Most of the Polynesian ones can be defined as more or less complex platform structures, as, e.g. the *ahu* on Easter Island, the *marae* in the Societies, the *heiau* in Hawaíi, the *langi* in Tonga, and also the *naga* in Fiji, the latter in Melanesia. There is today clear evidence that the religious monuments began as fairly simple structures, and that many of them later reached monumental status (Wallin 1993; Martinsson-Wallin 1994; Martinsson-Wallin 1998; Green 2000:88) (fig. 10-11).

Recent excavations have revealed important data for the interpretation of the emergence and subsequent development of this process. The earliest dates for ceremonial *ahu* platforms today available in east Polynesia comes from Easter Island, while dated *marae* structures further west, e.g. in the Society Islands, are later (Wallin 1993; Martinsson-Wallin 1994; Martinsson-Wallin & Wallin 1998). The first appearance of these megalithic structures seems, however, not associated with the initial landnam on the island. According to Martinsson-Wallin and Wallin (1998:183), the initial settlement on Easter Island took place between AD 800 and AD 1000, while the earliest *ahu* structures seem to have been built after AD 1100. Taking these dates into consideration, earlier theories on a South-American origin for the Easter Island population (e.g Heyerdahl 1965), based on similarities in monumental stone *moai* statues and stone-building techniques (*ahu* masonry), are again highlighted, but now from a completely new angle. While the initial Easter Island settlers undisputedly were Polynesians, arriving from the west, the development of, at least more complex, ceremonial structures may well later have been initiated from the civilizations in the Andes through long-distance contact and exchange of ideas. It has been argued, that the earliest, simple platform structures may have a Polynesian origin. However, the developed dressing and fitting of the stones in more monumental structures, as they appear on Easter Island in the 13th century AD, may well originate in South America (Emory 1943:11; Skjølsvold 1994; Green 2000:88). It is reasonable to believe that the sweet-potato and the white flower bottle gourd were introduced into the Pacific area at this stage (Green 1998, 2000:85, 94). The refinements in monumental stone building techniques, especially the fitting of masonry, then seem to have diffused westwards to the Society Islands and the rest of Polynesia in the 14th and 15th centuries AD (e.g. Smith 1961:248; Emory 1970; Wallin 1993; Green 1998).

At the time of the arrival of the first Europeans in the Pacific, notably Captain James Cook in the 1770's, well established long-distance contacts and trade networks were operating over vast areas, linking populations with frequent contacts at distances corresponding to the area of of the whole of Europe, including northern Africa and western Asia (Lewis 1972; Weisler 1998a). In fact, the area of Atlantic Europe from Norway to southern Portugal fits well into only one of a series of well documented, inter-linked areas of prehistoric Pacific around Fiji, Tonga and Samoa, limited by the Cook Islands in the east, Tuvalu in the North and Santa Cruz and Vanuatu in the west (fig. 12).

It seems reasonable to argue, that if the stone age populations all over the Pacific region had well documented close and regular contacts, shared a common world of material culture, religious beliefs, architectural and symbolic features, and also language group, surely we have to consider and investigate the possibilities of a similar situation in the comparatively small area along the Atlantic coasts. It should again be noted, that the Pacific interaction zones were established in an open ocean situation, where, in many cases, no land or island was available between the departure localities and the final destinations. Returning to our west European example, we suddenly realize that advanced seafaring really was not necessary in order to establish regular, long-distance networks along the Atlantic coasts and the Mediterranean area, although such skill undoubtedly must have existed also in Europe during the Neolithic. I would rather describe it as "coastal hopping" in most cases. In a prehistoric Pacific perspective, the European equivalent seems like walking around your own back yard. I would not be surprised if priests from the Maltese temples occasionally attended ceremonies at Newgrange – and the other way around. In any case, future research cannot exclude the possibility of such close contacts.

References

Anderson, A. 1994. The Occupation of the Pacific Islands. In: Burenhult, G. (ed.), *The Illustrated History of Humankind, Vol. 4, New World and Pacific Civilizations*. Sydney and Höganäs.

ApSimon, A. 1986. Chronological context for Irish megalithic tombs. *JIA* volume III.

Bellwood, P. 1989. The colonization of the Pacific: some current hypotheses. In A.V.S. Hill and S.W. Serjeantson (eds), *The Colonization of the Pacific: a Genetic Trail*. Oxford.

Bergh, S. 1995. *Landscape of the Monuments. A study of the passage tombs in the Cúil Irra region, Co. Sligo, Ireland*. Studier från UV, Stockholm. Arkeologiska undersökningar, Skrifter nr 6. Riksantikvarieämbetet.

Bradley, R. 1997. *Rock Art and the Prehistory of Atlantic Europe. Signing the Land*. London and New York.

Bradley, R. and Chapman, R. 1984. Passage graves in the European Neolithic – a theory of converging evolution. In: Burenhult, G., The Archaeology of Carrowmore. *Theses and Papers in North-European Archaeology* 14. University of Stockholm.

Burenhult, G. 1980a. The Archaeological Excavations at Carrowmore, Co. Sligo, Ireland. Excavation seasons 1977-79. *Theses and Papers in North-European Archaeology* 9. University of Stockholm.

Burenhult, G. 1980b. The Rock Carvings of Götaland, Part 1. *Theses and Papers in North-European Archaeology* 10. Dept. of Archaeology, University of Stockholm.

Burenhult, G. 1981. *Stenåldersbilder. Hällristningar och stenåldersekonomi. Hällbilder som samhällsdokument från sten- och bronsålder i Europa och Noradfrika 5000-500 f.Kr.* Stockholm.

Burenhult, G. 1984. The Archaeology of Carrowmore, Co. Sligo, Ireland. *Theses and Papers in North-European Archaeology* 14. University of Stockholm.

Burenhult, G. 1999. Megalithic Symbolism in Ireland and Scandinavia in light of new evidence from Carrowmore. In: Cruz, A.R. & Oosterbeek, L. (eds), Perspectiva em Diálogo. 1.° Curso Intensivo de Arte Pré-Histórica Europeia. Tomo I. *ARKEOS 6*. Tomar.

Burenhult, G. 2001. *The Illustrated Guide to the Megalithic Cemetery of Carrowmore, Co. Sligo*. New Revised Edition. Malmö.

Burenhult, G. in preparation. *Carrowmore revisited. Report from the Excavation Campaign 1994-1998*.

Burenhult, G. & Possnert, G. in preparation. *New Radiocarbon dates from Carrowmore Megalithic Cemetery, Co. Sligo, Ireland*.

Caulfield, S. 1983. The Neolithic Settlement of North Connaught. In: Reeves-Smyth, T. & Hamond, F. (eds), *Landscape Archaeology in Ireland*. BAR British Series 116.

Champion, T., Gamble, C., Shennan, S. & Whittle, A. 1984. *Prehistoric Europe*. London.

Chapman, R. 1981. The Megalithic Tombs of Iberia. In: Renfrew, C. (ed.), *The Megalithic Tombs of Western Europe*. London.

Clark, D. & Maguire, P. 1989. *Skara Brae*.

Cooney, G. 1990. The place of megalithic tomb cemeteries in Ireland. *Antiquity* 64.

Cooney, G. 2000. *Landscapes of Neolithic Ireland*. London.

Cooney, G. & Grogan, E. 1994. *Irish Prehistory – A social perspective*. Dublin.

Currán-Mulligan, P. 1994. Yes, but it is Art!. *Archaeology Ireland* 8:1.

Darvill, T. 1979. Court cairns, passage graves and social change in Ireland. *Man* 14.

Emory, K.P. 1933. *Stone Remains in the Society Islands*. Bernice P. Bishop Museum Bulletin 163. Honolulu.

Emory, K.P. 1943. Polynesian stone remains. In: Coon, C.S. & Andrews IV, J.M. (eds), *Studies in the Anthropology of Oceania and Asia, Presented in Memory of Roland Burrage Dixon*. Papers of the Peabody Museum of American Archaeology and Ethnology. Harvard University Vol. XX.

Emory, K.P. 1970. A re-examination of East Polynesian *marae*: Many *marae* later. In: Green, R.C. & Kelly, M. (eds), *Studies in Oceanic Culture History. Volume 1*. Pacific Anthropological Records 11. Honolulu: Bernice P. Bishop Museum.

Eogan, G. 1979. Objects with Iberian affinities from Knowth. *Revista de Gumaraes 89*.

Eogan, G. 1986. *Knowth and the passage tombs of Ireland*. London.

Evans, J.D. 1959. *Malta*. London.

Evans, J.D. 1971. *The prehistoric Antiquities of the Maltese Islands: A Survey*. London.

Fett, E.N. & Fett, P. 1980. Relations West Norway – Western Europe Documented in Petroglyphs. *N.A.R. Norwegian Archaeological Review*, Vol. 12, No. 2, 1979.

Finney, B.R. 1977. Voyaging canoes and the settlement of Polynesia. *Science 196*.

Glob, P.V. 1969. *Helleristninger i Danmark*. Copenhagen.

Gosden, C. 1991. Long term trends in the colonization of the Pacific: putting Lapita in its place. *Bulletin of the Indo-Pacific Prehistory Association 11*.

Gosden, C. 1992. Production systems and colonization of the Western Pacific. *World Archaeology 24(1)*.

Gosden, C. 1993. Relics of the first New Ireland settlers. In: Burenhult, G. (ed.), *The Illustrated History of Humankind, Volume 1. The First Humans. Human Origins and History to 10,000 BC*. Sydney and Höganäs.

Green, R.C. 1993. Tropical Polynesian prehistory-where are we now? In M. Spriggs, D.E. Yen, W. Ambrose, R. Jones, A. Thorne and A. Andrews (eds.), A *Community of Culture: The People and Prehistory of the Pacific*. Department of Prehistory, Research School of Pacific Studies, Australain National University, Canberra, Occasional Papers in Prehistory No. 21.

Green, R.C. 1998. Rapanui origins prior to European contact – the view from Eastern Polynesia. In: Vargas Casanova, P. (ed.), *Easter Island and East Polynesian Prehistory*. Santiago: Instituto de Estudios Isla de Pascua, Facultad de Arquitectura y Urbanismo, Universidad de Chile.

Green, R.C. 2000. Religious Structures of Southeastern Polynesia: Even More Marae Later. In: Wallin, P. & Martinsson-Wallin, H. (eds), *Essays in Honour of Arne Skjølsvold 75 years*. The Kon-Tiki Museum Occasional Papers, Volume 5. Oslo.

Grogan E, 1991. Radiocarbon dates from Brugh na Bóinne. In: Eogan, G. Prehistoric and Early Historic culture change at Brugh na Bóinne. *Proceedings of the Royal Irish Academy* 91C.

Hagen, A. 1969. Studier i vestnorsk bergkunst. Ausevik i Flora. *Årb. F. Univ. I Bergen 1969*. Bergen.

Heyerdahl, T. 1965. The statues of the Oipona *Me'ae*, with a comparative analysis of possibly related stone monuments. In: Heyerdahl, T. & Ferdon Jr, E. (eds), *Reports of the Norwegian Archaeological Expedition to Easter Island and the East Pacific, Volume 2. Miscellaneous Papers*. Monographs of the School of American Research and the Kon-Tiki Museum 24, part 2. Stockholm.

Irwin, G. 1980. The prehistory of Oceania: colonization and culture change. In A. Sherratt (ed.), *The Cambridge Encyclopedia of Archaeology*. Cambridge.

Irwin, G. 1990. Human colonisation and change in the remote Pacific. *Current Anthropology 31*.

Irwin, G., Bickler, S. & Quirke, P. 1990. Voyaging by canoe and computer: experiments in the settlement of the Pacific Ocean. *Antiquity 64*.

Lewis, D. 1972. *We, the Navigators*. Canberra.

Montelius, O. 1905. *Orienten och Europa*. Antiqvarisk Tidskrift för Sverige, B XIII. Stockholm.

Martinsson-Wallin, H. 1994. *Ahu – The Ceremonial Stone Structures of Easter Island*. AUN 19. Uppsala.

Martinsson-Wallin H. & Wallin, P. 1998. Excavations at Anakena. The Easter island settlement sequence and change of subsistence. In: Vargas Casanova, P. (ed.), *Easter Island and East Polynesian Prehistory*. Santiago: Instituto de Estudios Isla de Pascua, Facultad de Arquitectura y Urbanismo, Universidad de Chile.

Müller-Karpe, H. 1974. *Handbuch der Vorgeschichte, Band III:1-3*. München.

O'Kelly, M.J. 1981. The Megalithic Tombs of Ireland. In: Evans, J.D., Cunliffe, B. and Renfrew, C. (eds): *Antiquity and Man. Essays in Honour of Glyn Daniel*. London.

O'Kelly, M.J. 1982. *Newgrange: Archaeology, art and legend*. London and New York.

Péquart, M. & Le Rouzic, Z. 1927. *Corpus des signes gravés des monuments mégalitiques du Morbihan*. Paris.

Renfrew, C. 1973. *Before Civilization. The Radiocarbon Revolution and Prehistoric Europe*. New York.

Savory, H.N. 1968. *Spain and Portugal*. London.

Shee Twohig, E. 1981. *The Megalithic Art of Western Europe*. Oxford.

Sheridan, A. 1985/6. Megaliths and Megalomania: An account, and interpretation, of the development of passage tombs in Ireland. *JIA 3*.

Skjølsvold, A. 1994. Archaeological investigations at Anakena, Easter Island. In: Skjølsvold, A. (ed.) *Archaeological Investigations at Anakena, Easter Island*. The Kon-Tiki Museum Occasional Papers 3:5. Oslo.

Smith, C.S. 1961. A temporal sequence derived from certain ahu. In: Heyerdahl, T. & Ferdon Jr, E. (eds), *Reports of the Norwegian Archaeological Expedition to Easter Island and the East Pacific, Volume 1, Archaeology of Easter Island*. Monographs of the School of American Research and the Museum of New Mexico 24. Santa Fe.

Spriggs, M. 1999. Pacific Archaeologies: Contested Ground in the Construction of Pacific History. *The Journal of Pacific History, Vol. 34, No. 1*.

Thorpe, I.J. 1996. *The Origins of Agriculture in Europe*. London and New York.

Trump, D.H. 1966. *Southern Italy before Rome*. London.

Trump, D.H. 1972. *Archaeological Guide to Malta*. London.

Trump, D., Bonanno, A., Gouder, T., Malone, C. & Stoddart, S. 1993. New Light on Death in

Prehistoric Malta: The Brochtorff Circle. In: Burenhult, G. (ed.), *The Illustrated History of Humankind, Volume 2. People of the Stone Age. Hunter-gatherers and Early farmers*. Sydney and Höganäs.

Waddell, J. 1998. *The Prehistoric Archaeology of Ireland*. Galway.

Wallin, P. 1993. *Ceremonial Stone Structures: The Archaeology and Ethnohistory of the Marae Complex in the Society Islands, French Polynesia*. AUN 18. Uppsala.

Weisler, M. 1998a. Hard evidence for prehistoric interaction in Polynesia. *Current Anthropology, 39*.

Weisler, M. 1998b. Issues in the colonization and settlement of Polynesian islands. In: Vargas Casanova, P. (ed.), *Easter Island and East Polynesian Prehistory*. Santiago: Instituto de Estudios Isla de Pascua, Facultad de Arquitectura y Urbanismo, Universidad de Chile.

White, J.P. 1993. The First Pacific Islanders. In: Burenhult, G. (ed.) *The Illustrated History of Humankind, Volume 1*. In: Burenhult, G. (ed.), *The Illustrated History of Humankind, Volume 1. The First Humans. Human Origins and History to 10,000 BC*. Sydney and Höganäs.

Wilson, J. 1799. *A Missionary Voyage to the South Pacific Ocean, Performed on the Years 1796, 1797, 1798, on the Ship Duff, Commanded by Captain James Wilson Under the Direction of the Missionary Society*. London.

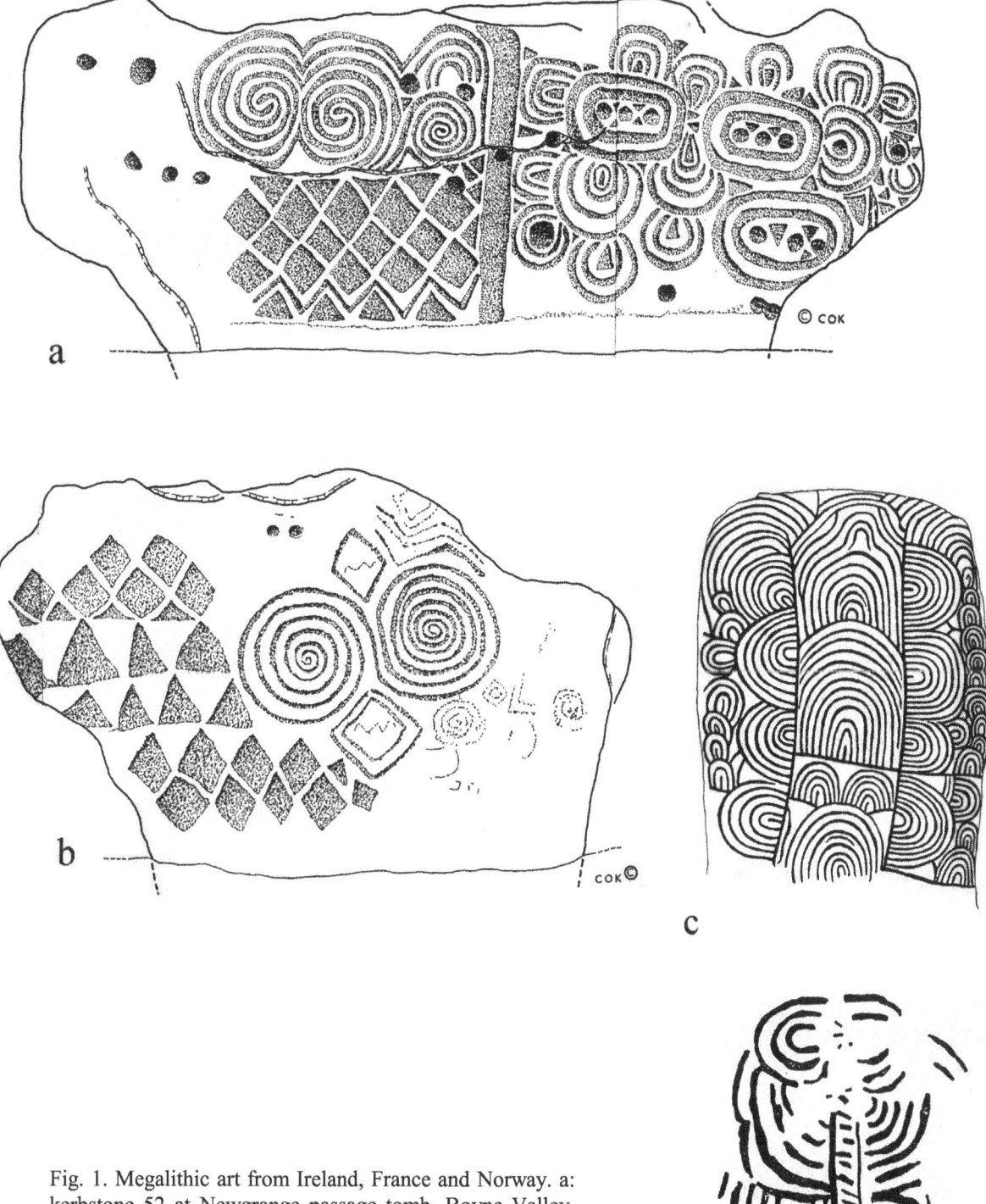

Fig. 1. Megalithic art from Ireland, France and Norway. a: kerbstone 52 at Newgrange passage tomb, Boyne Valley, Ireland; b: kerbstone 67 at Newgrange passage tomb, Boyne Valley, Ireland; c: decorated stone from Gavrinis passage tomb, Brittany, France; d: rock-carving from western Norway, Ausevik No. 261. a-b after O'Kelly 1982; c after Péquart & Le Rouzic 1927; d after Hagen 1969.

Cultural Interactions in Europe and the Eastern Mediterranean during the Bronze Age (3000-500 BC)

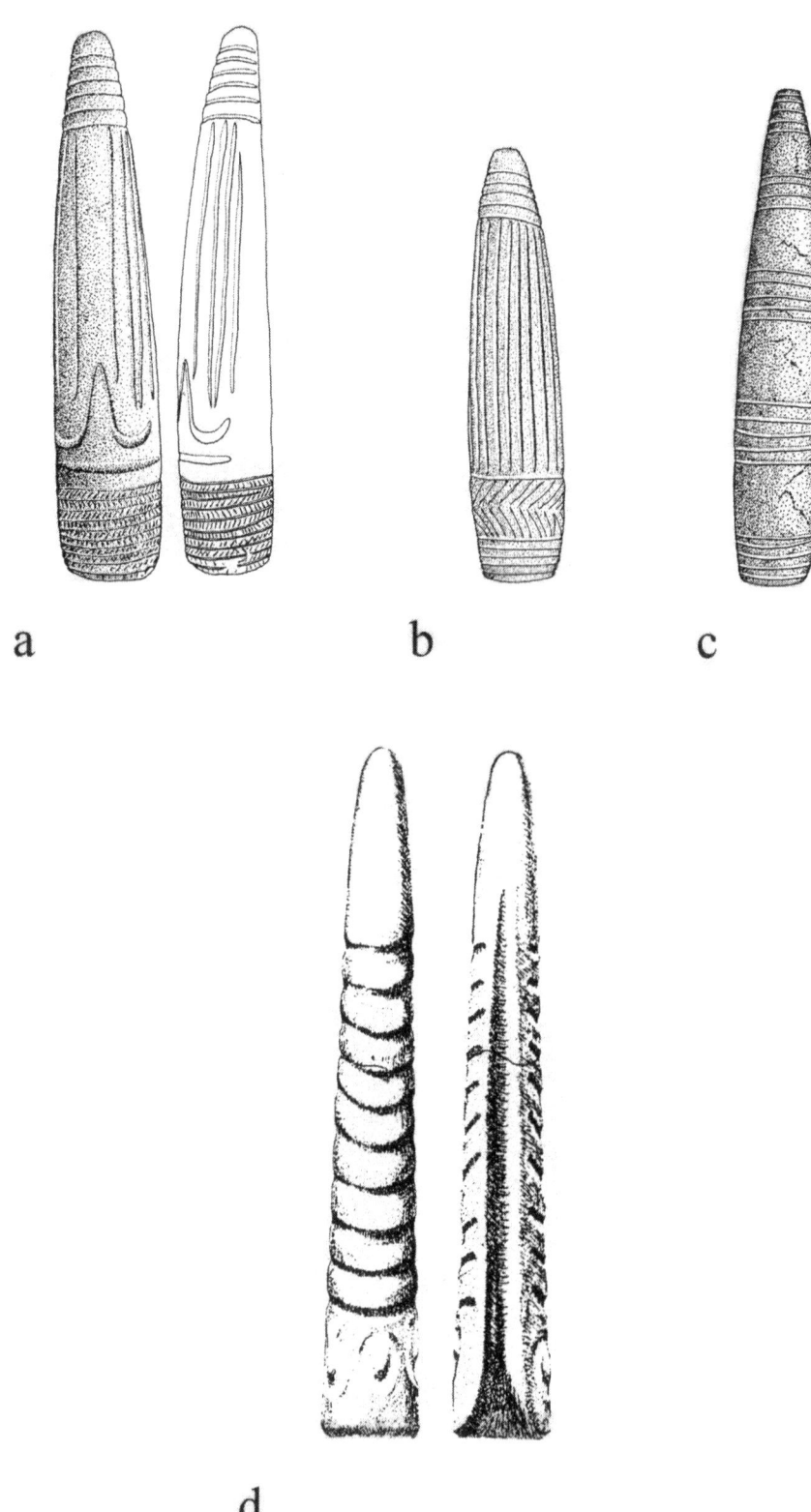

Fig. 2. Pointed sandstone, half-cylinder objects from various megalithic tombs in Ireland and Portugal. a: Casainhos, Estremadura, Portugal; b: Palmela, Estremadura, Portugal; c: Carenque-Baútas, Estremadura, Portugal, d: Knowth passage tomb, Boyne Valley, Ireland. a-c after Müller-Karpe 1974; d: after Eogan 1986.

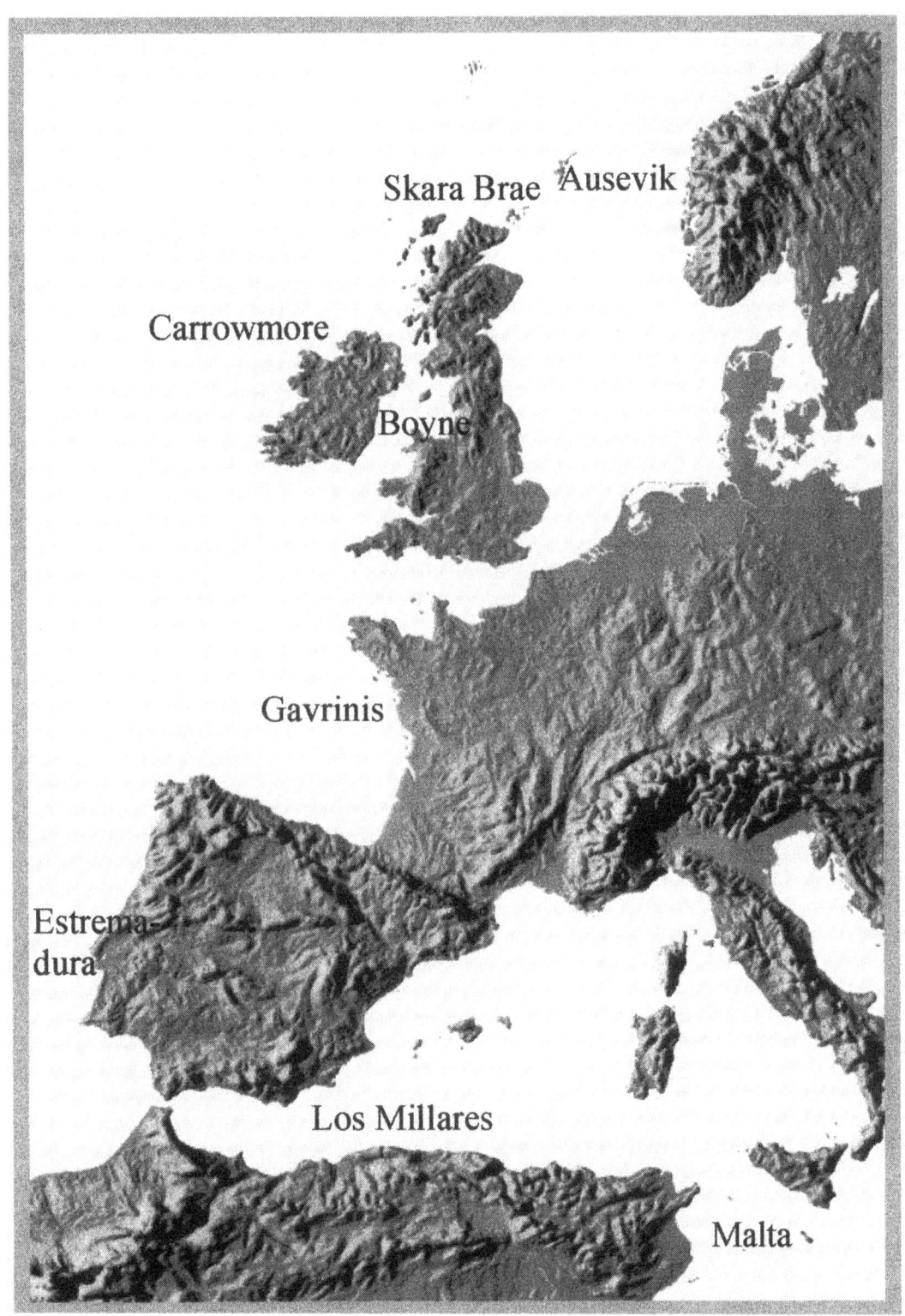

Fig. 3. Map of Atlantic Europe and the western Mediterranean area. Sites mentioned in the text have been marked.

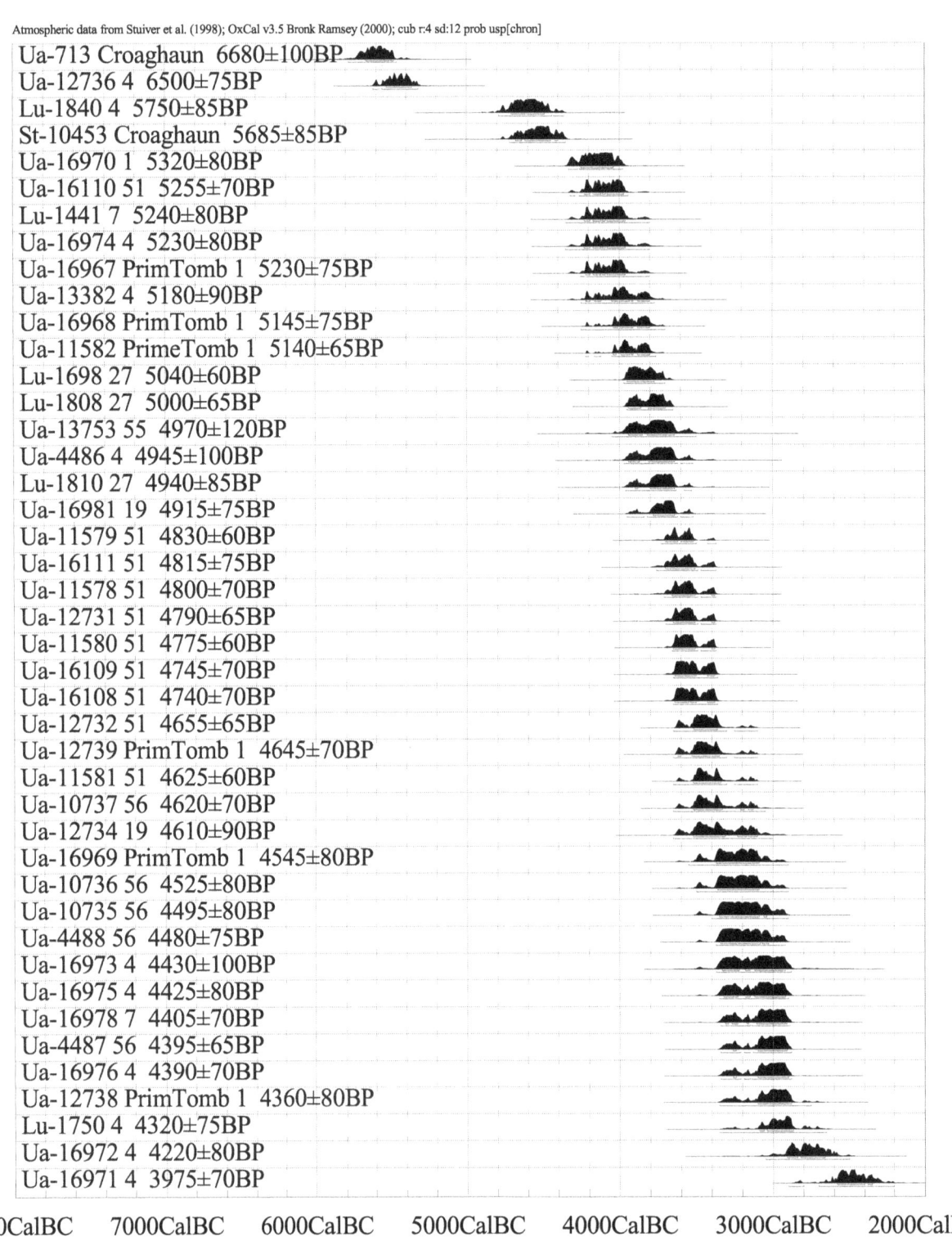

Fig. 4. Calibrated radiocarbon dates from Carrowmore megalithic cemetery, Primrose Grange Tomb No. 1, and Croaghaun, Co. Sligo, Ireland. Diagram compiled by Göran Possnert, The Ångström Laboratory, Uppsala University, Sweden.

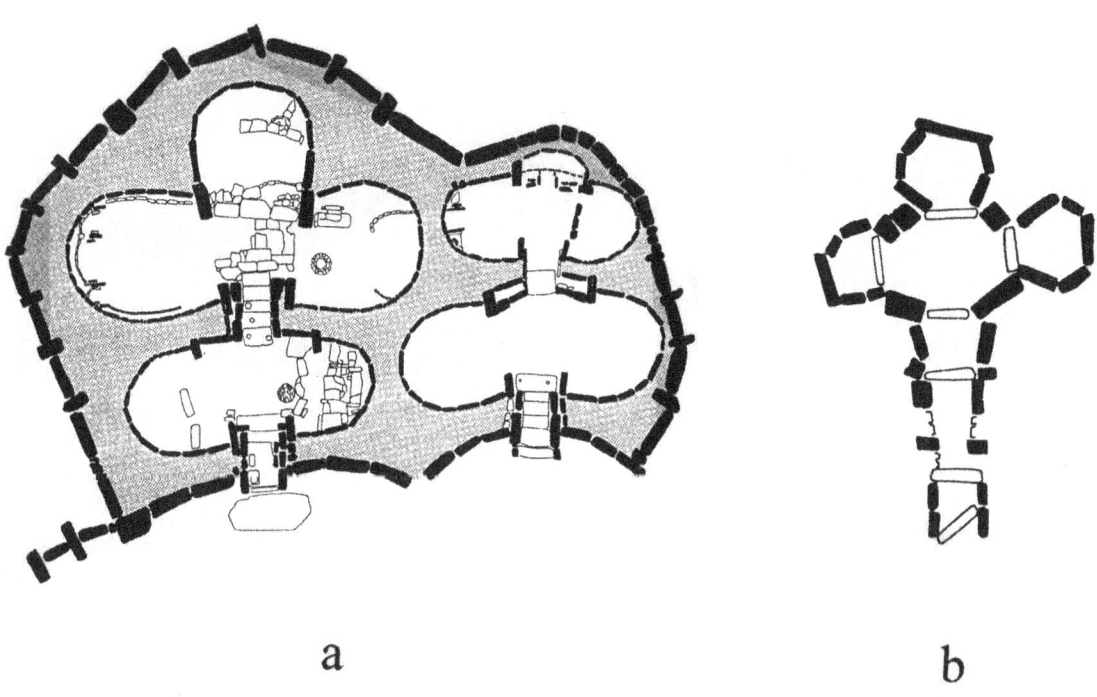

Fig. 5. Plans of megalithic structures from Ireland and Malta. a: Ggantija temple, Gozo, Malta; b: passage tomb at Carrowkeel megalithic cemetery, Co. Sligo, Ireland. a-b after Müller-Karpe 1974.

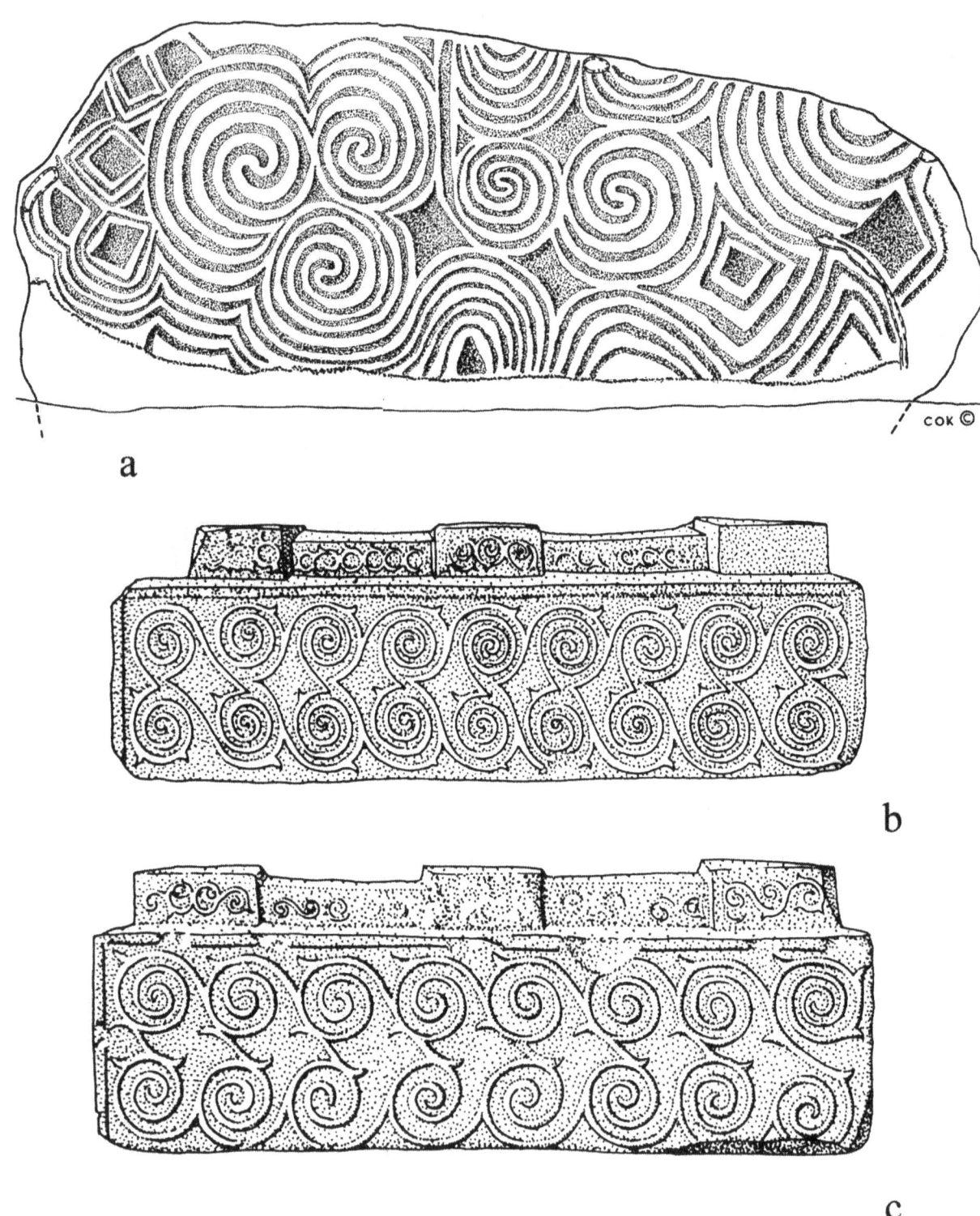

Fig. 6. Decorated stones from Ireland and Malta. a: kerbstone 1 at Newgrange passage tomb, Boyne Valley, Ireland; b-c: Tarxien temple. Malta. a after O'Kelly 1982; b-c after Müller-Karpe 1974.

Fig. 7. Examples of surface dressing on stones in megalithic structures from Malta and Ireland. a-b: Hagar Qim temple, Malta; c: stone R21 at Newgrange, Boyne Valley, Ireland. a-b after Müller-Karpe 1974; c after O'Kelly 1982.

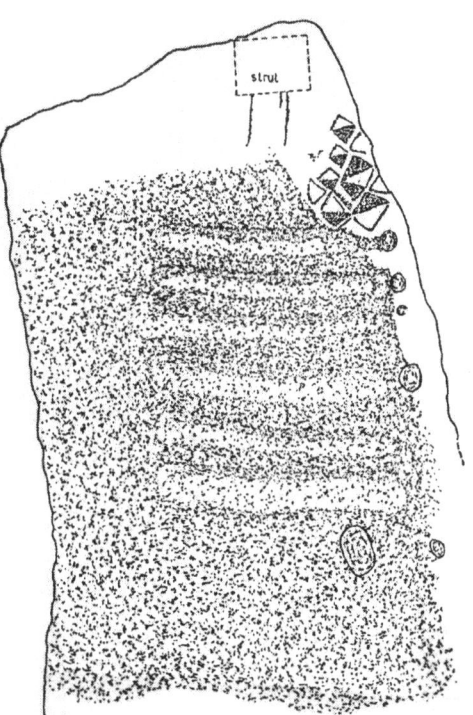

Cultural Interactions in Europe and the Eastern Mediterranean during the Bronze Age (3000-500 BC)

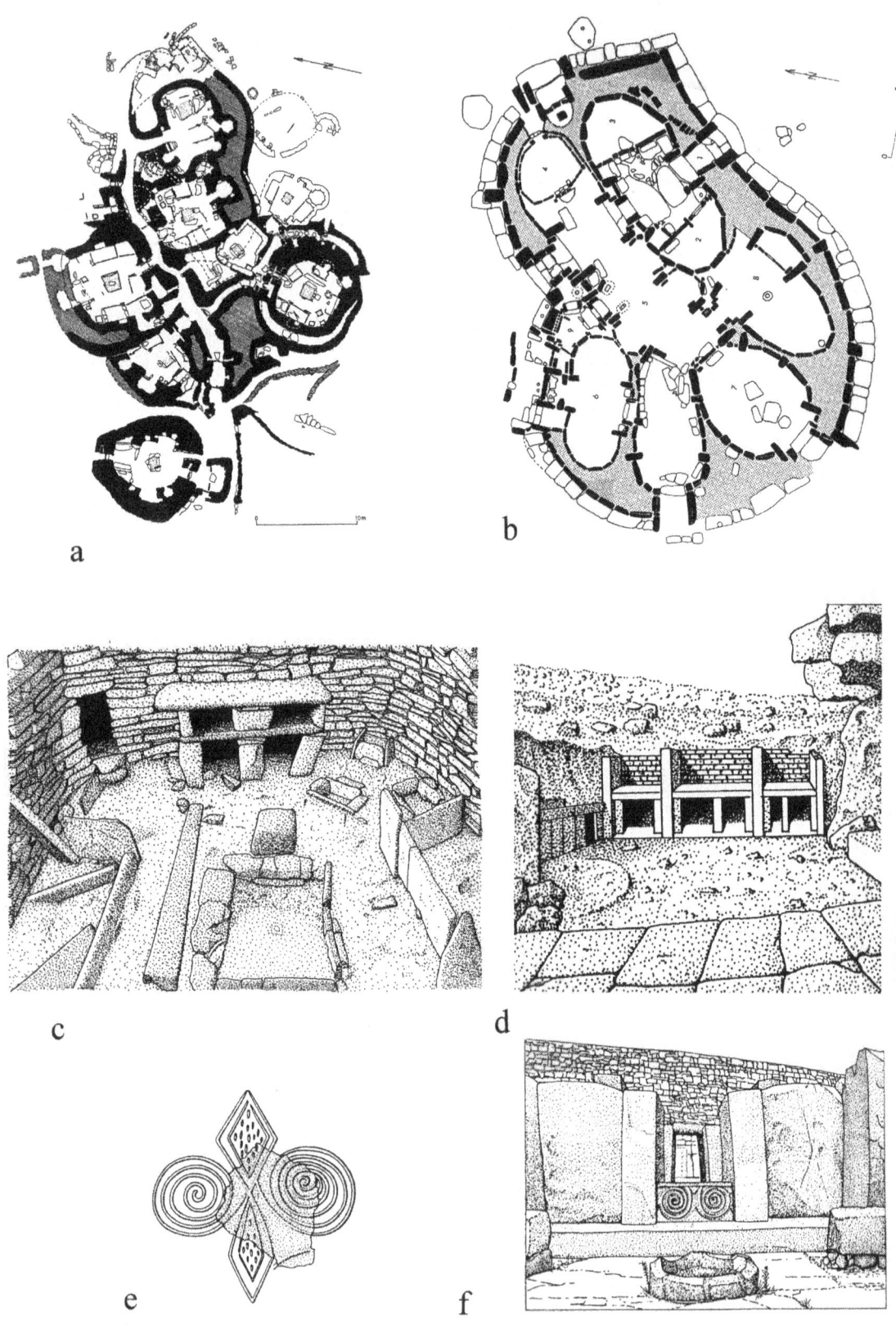

Fig. 8. Architectural and symbolic features from Orkney and Malta. a: ground plan of the Skara Brae houses, Orkney; b: plan of Hagar Qim temple, Malta; c: room interior from Skara Brae, Orkney, House 7, with stone-built dressers, hearths, stone-lined structures, tables, cupboards and nisches; d: room interior from Ggantija temple, Malta, with apses, nisches and altars; e: potsherd from Skara Brae, Orkney, decorated with a double spiral; f: room interior from Tarxien temple, with apses, nisches, stone-lined structure on the floor and an altar, decorated with a double spiral. a-f after Müller-Karpe 1974.

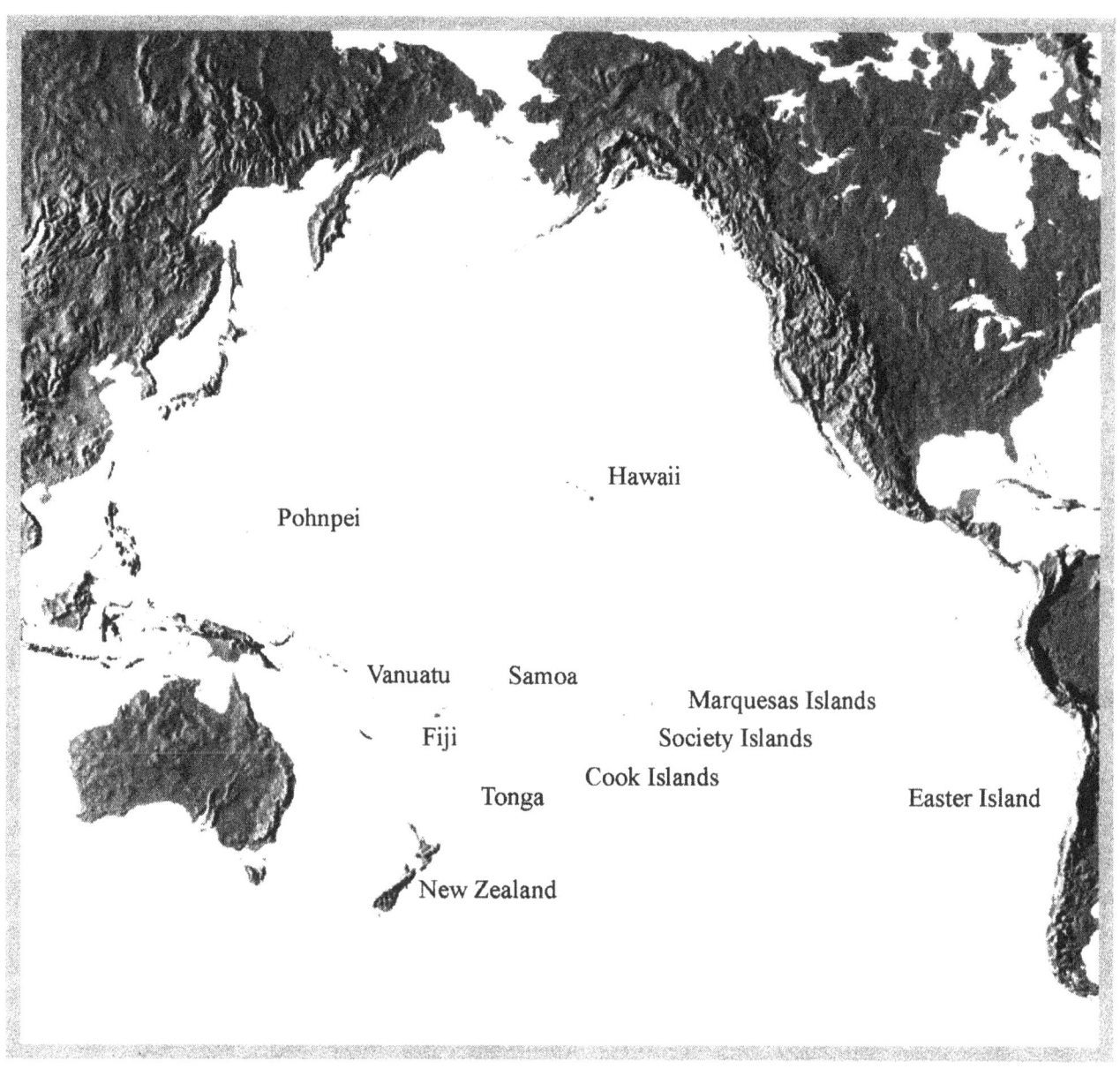

Fig. 9. Map of the Pacific Ocean with major megalithic centres marked.

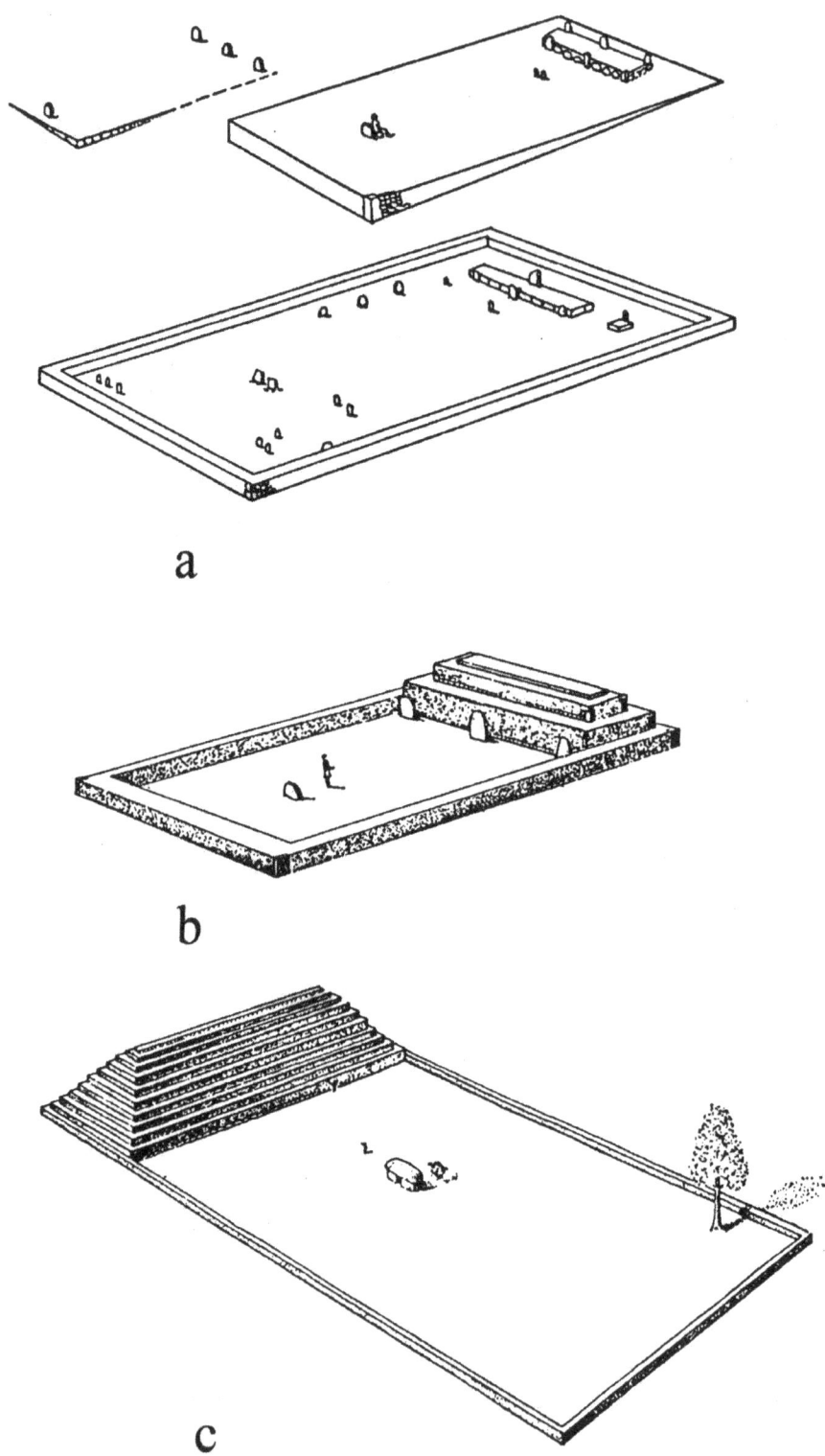

Fig. 10. The development of *marae* structures in the Society Islands (Tahiti and Mo'orea). a: the simplest version, a paved court with a shrine-like architectural feature, mostly found in in-land positions; b: stepped-platform *marae*, typical of those found along the coasts; c: the ten-step Mahaiatea *marae* on Tahiti. After Emory 1933.

Göran Burenhult: Long-distance cultural interaction in megalithic Europe

Fig. 11. *Marae* Mahaiatea on Tahiti, Papara district, in 1797. After Wilson 1799.

Cultural Interactions in Europe and the Eastern Mediterranean during the Bronze Age (3000-500 BC)

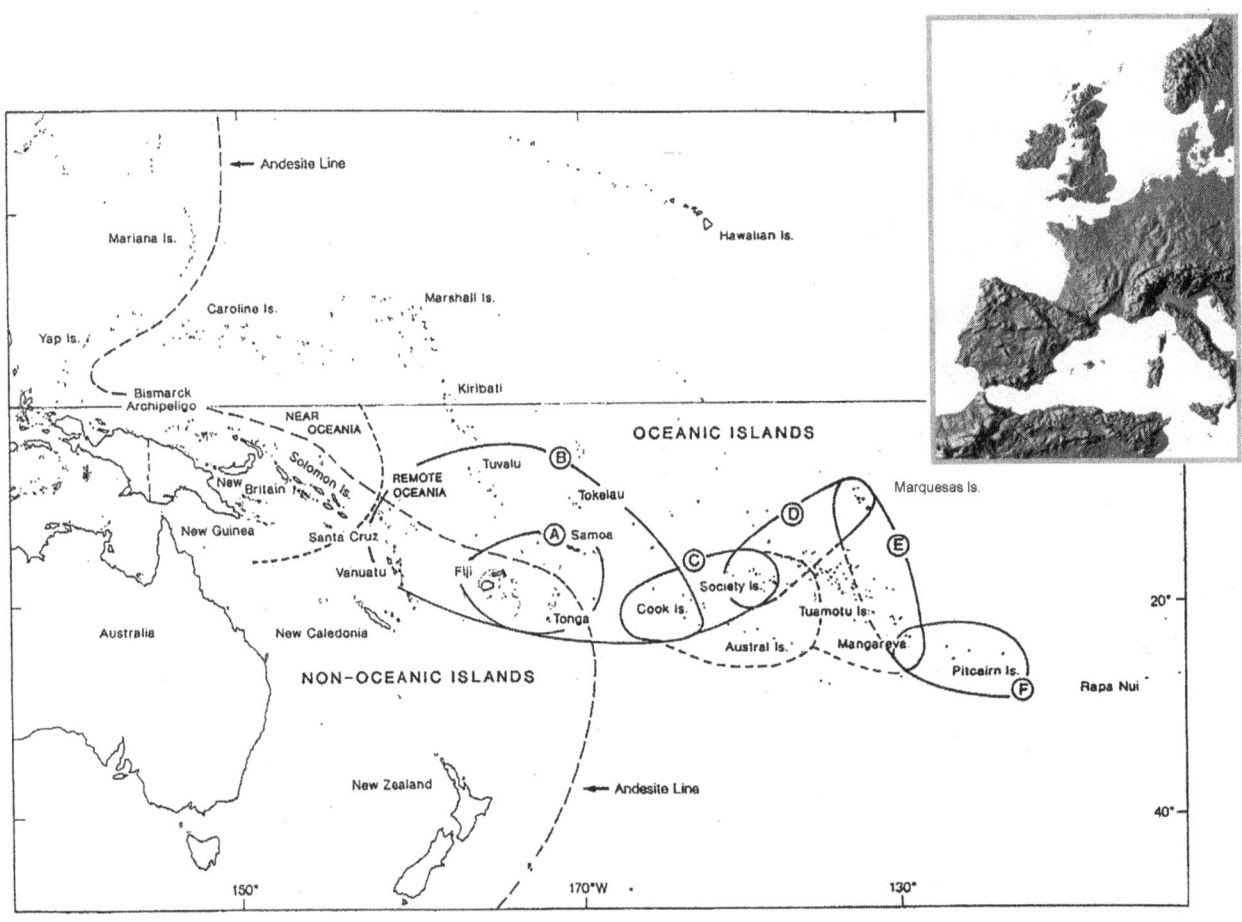

Fig. 12. Archaeologically and ethnohistorically documented interaction spheres in the Pacific. Solid lines denote known interaction regions, dashed lines suspected ones. A is based on ethnohistoric sources, B through F are defined by archaeological transfers of fine-grained basalt adze materials. (After Weisler 1998a and Green 2000). To allow for a distance comparison, a map of Atlantic Europe and the western Mediterranean has been scaled into the Pacific area.

Sappho's Poetry and Ancient Egyptian Love Poems: A Field of Comparative Interpretation, 2

Amanda–Alice Maravelia

Abstract

In a former paper an attempt has been made towards understanding the latent, yet evident, common points between some Sapphic fragments and their ancient Egyptian equivalent lyrics. A preliminary explanation of the influences that Sappho probably received was given, together with concomitant commentaries. Twelve cases of common attributes/symbols were then specified and analysed. It was assumed that these (well assimilated) influences were characteristic of the general Mediterranean literary interactions and cultural exchanges, which were taking place slowly although steadily from South to North (hence from Egypt towards Greece), and vice versa. In the present paper, the analysis is reprised afresh, new instances are examined, and a useful table of all the related passages, from both Egyptian and Greek texts is presented for immediate comparison. This consists a useful tool in interpreting further the interesting phenomenon of homoeogenetic feedback between two ancient nations of the Mediterranean basin.

KEY WORDS: Egypt: Ancient Egyptian Love Songs; Greece: Sappho, Sapphic Lyrics; Mediterranean Cultural Interactions.

I. Introduction

Poetry is *par excellence* The Art of heart and feeling, which vibrates through the brain filters and comes out as a pure conception of light and life. Hence, presumably great poetry must and can assimilate various elements which enrich her and make of her a true living body, which transforms the material food into energy and thought. This is the case for Sappho's lyrics, which holds also for the ancient Egyptian love poems[1], and in this context the assumptions and analysis of the present paper must be considered. Regrettably, the number of the extant fragments of Sappho's lyrics is not directly proportional to the poetic *grandeur* of their content. Several attempts have been already made towards their presentation and classification[2], the most outstanding of them being those by

---

[1] The most important of the known sources of ancient Egyptian love poems are the following: (i) *pHarris 500* (= BM n° 10060), r, pp. I, l. 1 - VI, l. 2 & pp. VII, l. 3 - VIII, l. 12; initially published by Maspero, G.: "Les Chants d'amour du Papyrus de Turin et du Papyrus Harris n° 500", *Études égyptiennes*, I, Paris (Maisonneuve) 1883, pp. 217-59; the original (transcription into hieroglyphs) used in this paper was published by Müller, W.M.: *Die Liebespoesie der Alten Ägypter*, Leipzig (J.C. Hinrichs'sche Buchhandlung) 1899, plates. 2-16. (ii) *pTurin 1996* (= CGTurin n° 1966), r, pp. I, l. 1 - II, l. 15; initially published as mentioned in (i); see also Scamuzzi, E.: *Museo Egizio di Torino*, Torino 1963, pl. 89 and Scamuzzi, E.: *L'art égyptien au Musée de Turin*, Paris (Hachette) 1966, pl. LIV; the original (transcription into hieroglyphs) used in this paper was published by Fox, M.V.: *The Song of Songs and the Ancient Egyptian Love Songs*, Madison WI (University of Wisconsin Press) 1985, pp. 389-93; for another interesting edition of this papyrus see Lopez, J.: "Le verger d'amour (P. Turin 1966, recto)", *RdE*, **43**, 1992, pp. 133-43. (iii) *pChester Beatty I* (= BM n° 10681), v, pp. C1, l. 1 - C5, l. 2 & pp. G1, l. 1 - G2, l. 5 & r, pp. 16, l. 9 - 17, l. 13; initially published by Gardiner, A.H.: *The Library of A. Chester Beatty. The Chester Beatty Papyri, No I*, London (Oxford University Press) 1931, pp. 1-7 & 27-38 & plates XXII-XXVI (= verso, section C), XXIX-XXX (= verso, section G), XVI-XVII (=recto); this edition was used here. (iv) *oDeM 1266 + oCG25218*, ll. 1-28; initially published in whole by Posener, G.: *Catalogue des ostraca hiératiques, littéraires de Deir el-Médineh, N°ˢ 1227–1266*, II[3], Caire (Publications de l'*Institut Français d'Archéologie Orientale*) 1972, pp. 43-4 & plates 75-9; this edition was used here. (v) *oGardiner 304*, r, ll. 1-7 & *oNash 12*, r, ll. 1-5; initially published by Černy, J. and Gardiner, A.H.: *Hieratic Ostraca*, I, Oxford (*Griffith Institute*, University Press) 1957, p. 11 & plates XXXVIII: 2, 26, and p. 12 & plates XL: 6, 26, respectively; this edition was used here. (vi) *oBorchardt 1*, r, ll. 1-9 + v, ll. 1-4 (= *oCGTurin 57367*, r); initially published by Lopez, J.: *Ostraca ieratici. Catalogo del Museo Egizio di Torino. Serie seconda. Collezioni (oCGT57320-57449)*, III/3, Milano 1982, p. 22 ff & plates 114-114a, 25; also published by Mathieu, B.: *La poésie amoureuse de l'Égypte ancienne. Recherches sur un genre littéraire au Nouvel Empire*, Paris (I.F.A.O., Bibliothèque d'Étude, **115**) 1996, pp. 113 4, plates 22-3, 24; the second edition was used here. (vii) *sLouvre C100*, ll. 1-4; initially published by Müller: *op. cit.*, 1899, plates. 16 & 18. (viii) *oDeM 1078* r+v, see Posener, G.: *Catalogue des ostraca hiératiques, littéraires de Deir el-Medinéh, N°ˢ 1001–1108*, I[1], Caire (Publications de l'*Institut Français d'Archéologie Orientale*) 1938, p. 20 & pl. 44; for *oDeM1079* + *oGardiner 339*, see ibid.: *op. cit.*, p. 20 ff & pl. 44; and Černy & Gardiner, *op. cit.*, p. 13 & pl. XLIII, 1; those editions were used here. For the rest of the sources see Mathieu: *op. cit.*, 1996, pp. 115-9, passim.

[2] Sappho's fragments have been published by the following authors: Edmonds, J.M.: *Lyra Graeca*, I, London and NY (Loeb) ²1928 (this being the main source in the present paper); Bergk, T.: *Poetae Lyrici Graeci*, Lipsiae (Sumtu Reichenbachiorum Fratrum) 1843; Bowra, C.M.: *Greek Lyric Poetry*, Oxford (Oxford at the Clarendon Press) ²1961, pp. 176-240; for Alkaios see pp. 130-75; Lobel, E.: *Saphous Melê*, Oxford (Oxford at the Clarendon Press) 1925; Lobel, E. and Page, D.: *Poetarum Lesbiorum Fragmenta*, Oxford (Oxford at the Clarendon Press) 1963; Barnstone, W.: *Sappho*, NY (Anchor Books) 1965; Treu, M.: *Sappho. Lieder*, München (Tusculum) ⁶1979; Diehl, E.: *Anthologia Lyrica Graeca*, I, Leipzig 1935. For excellent translations and commentaries, see Barnard, M.: *Sappho* (new translation; foreword by Fitts, D.), CA (University of CA Press) 1966; Battistini, Y.: *Lyra erotica*, Paris (Imprimerie Nationale) 1992; Haines, C.R.: *Sappho. The Poems and Fragments*, London (RKP) 1926; Wharton, H.T.: *Sappho. Memoir, Text, Selected Renderings and a Literal Translation*, London (John Lane) 1898. For Sappho's editions, together with other ancient Greek lyric poets see also Rable, P.–P.: *Anacreôn–Sapphô*, Paris 1855; and Wilamowitz–Möllendorf, V. von: *Sappho und Simonides. Untersuchungen über Griechische Lyriker*, Berlin (Weidmannsche Buchhandlung) 1913. For Theokritos (a compa-rative reference to whom is found in Table 1, II[D].1, 12 & footnote 23) and his work see Gow, A.S.F. (ed., transl. & com.): *Theokritus*, I-II, Cambridge (Cambridge University Press) 1950, especially I: p. 116 & II: p. 293. Finally, two very good translations into modern Greek (actually that by Elytês attempts an imaginary restitution of the extant fragments with considerable success) are the following: Elytês, O.: *Sappho. Restitution and Translation*, Athens (Ikaros) ²1985; and Kakisês, S.: *Sappho. The Poems*, Athens (Kedros) ⁵1986.

Lobel, Edmonds, Lobel and Page, Bowra, Barnstone, & c., while the very fact of their inhomogeneous numbering is also to be noted. A synthesis of numbering, with emphasis on Edmonds' *Lyra*, will be followed here.

In a previous related paper [Maravelia, 2001], the plausible ways of possible influence of the Egyptian Love Poems[3] on Sappho's lyrics, in the general background of cultural interactions within the Mediterranean basin, during the reign of the Psametich's XXVI Dynasty, have been discussed[4]. In that paper, the most probable ways through which Sappho might have been influenced, have been examined, viz: her close relation with her brother Charaxos, who was visiting Egypt for trade and had a Graeco–Egyptian concubine, named Doricha; her relation to poet Alkaios who visited Egypt and stayed there; her exile to Sicily, Magna Graecia, and the assimilation of more cultural interactions there; finally, the fact that both Sappho and the poets of the ancient Egyptian Love Poems, belonged (or at least were closely related) to a courtesan, aristocratic milieu, trying to pray in sometimes similar ways the Erôs/*mrwt* and their matron deities Aphrodite/Hathor[5], because similar backgrounds create similar products as a *homoeogenesis procedure*.

Twelve cases of common poetical loci, and/or similar attributes were detected in that previous paper [Maravelia, 2001], after the comparative study of the known ancient Egyptian love poems —as they were published by Mathieu and Maravelia[6]— against the extant fragments of Sappho's lyrics. Their thematology had as follows: II.1. Golden Aphrodite/Golden Hathor Invocation; II.2. A Lonely Woman in Nocturnal Arousal; II.3. The Best Star/Sothis; II.4. The Heart–Broken and Afraid Girl; II.5. The Bitterness of Abandonment; II.6. The Luxury of Female's

---

[3] Maravelia, A.-A.: "Sappho's Poetry and Ancient Egyptian Love Poems: A Field of Comparative Interpre-tation, 1", *Proceedings of the XIth International Conference of the F.I.E.C.*, (Kalamakis, D., Manafis, K. & Vlachos, P., eds.), **I**, Athens (Parnassos) 2001, in press. A former, although rudimentary, comparative work, presented at a time where not all the Love Poems (or at least not so many as have been detected since today) were known, is that by Dornseiff, F.: "Ägyptische Liebeslieder, Hoheslied, Sappho, Theokrit", *Zeitschr. Dt. Morgenl. Ges.*, **90**, 1931, pp. 588-601 [republished in *Kleine Schriften, I: Antike und Alter Orient*, Leipzig (Köler & Amelang) 1956, pp. 189-202]. Dornseiff's work was very superficial and did not present more than a couple of cases, without comparative examination of the texts mentioned, whereas he was mainly interested in the interrelations between the *Old Testament* and Greek texts (Theokrito's idyls, & c.). For the influence of Sappho upon later authors, see Robinson, D.M.: *Sappho and her Influence*, NY 1963.

[4] For a background concerning the cultural interactions in the Mediterranean basin and Greece, see Faure, P.: *Die Griechische Welt im Zeitalter der Kolonisation*, Stuttgart 1981. See also the interesting book by Weigall, A.: *Sappho of Lesbos. Her Life and Times*, London (Thornton Butter-worth Ltd.) ²1937, especially chapters XVII: "The Greeks in Egypt" & VII: "Sappho's Exile in Sicily". For the Saitic Period and the relations of Greeks and Egyptians during that era, see also Lloyd, A.B.: "The Late Period", *Ancient Egypt: A Social History* (Trigger, B.G., *et al.*, eds.), Cambridge 1985, pp. 285-6, 294. Cf. also Grimal, N.: *A History of Ancient Egypt* (Shaw, I., transl.), Oxford (Blakwell) ²1992, pp. 363-4. The exile of Sappho took place during the reign of Psametichus II (595-89 BCE). When Charaxos, her brother, met the beautiful Doricha from Samos (aka Rhodopis), in Naukratis, he was 44, while the poetess 46. Sappho was totally opposed to that relation, because of her aristocratic ideals. It is to be noted that *LG 36* (cf. Table 1, II^D.11), a part of which is examined here, was written as a supplication of Sappho to Aphrodite, in order that her brother ends his relation with Doricha. Despite all these, he went again in Egypt, freed her and married her, which made Sappho very upset. On Sappho and her brother cf. also Dornseiff: "Ägyptische Liebeslieder ...", *Kleine Schriften*, 1956, pp. 189-90. See, also Weigall: *Sappho of Lesbos ...*, ²1937, chapter XVIII: "Sappho and Rhodopis the Courtesan". The same author argues (p. 220) that Sappho might have borrowed the *plêktron* from Egypt, where it is depicted in wall paintings from many tombs, and introduced it in Lesbos, using it in the musical support of her lyrics. Concerning the *plêktron* in ancient Egypt and concomitant paintings depicting musicians, see Manniche, L.: *Music and Musicians in Ancient Egypt*, London (BMP) 1991, pp. 46, 48. Weigall also states that the Sapphic metre reminds of some Northern African drum–tones. This might be possible, for the peculiar rhythm of Sappho's metre is similar *mutatis mutandis* to some Egyptian folk tones. For this metre see Irigoin, J.: "Côlon, vers et strophe dans la lyrique monodique grecque", *Rév. d. Phil*, **XXXI**, 1957. The conclusions of Mathieu, B.: "Études de métrique égyptienne: I. Le distique heptamètrique dans les chants d'amour", *RdE*, **39**, 1988, pp. 63-82, which are reprised in his PhD Thesis (Mathieu: *La poésie amoureuse ...*, 1996, pp. 202-3), concerning the basic heptametric structural unit of the ancient Egyptian strophes, might have been paralleled and compared to Sappho's metric, should the true vocalization of the ancient Egyptian language was known.

[5] The corresponding Egyptian term describing/defining the Egyptian Love Poems is either *hswt shmh ib* (*pHarris 500*, r, IV, l. 1 & VII, l. 3); either *rw nw t3 shmht-ib ʿ3t* (*pChester Beatty I*, v, C1, l.1); or *tsy ndmw* (*pChester Beatty I*, r, 16, l. 9). Hathor was considered as the goddess of love, fertility, and mistress of music and dance, hence she could be considered as the Egyptian analogue of the Greek goddess Aphrodite. See for instance, Manniche: *Music...*, 1991, pp. 12, 57, 60-68, passim. For Hathor see Helck, W., *et al.* (eds.): *Lexikon der Ägyptologie*, **II**, Wiesbaden (O. Harrassowitz) 1977, cols. 1024-33: art. "Hathor". See also Bleeker, C.J.: *Hathor and Thoth. Two Key Figures of the Ancient Egyptian Religion*, Leiden (Brill) 1973; and Bleeker, C.J.: "Isis and Hathor, Two Ancient Egyptian Goddesses", *The Book of the Goddess. Past and Present* (Olson, C., ed.), NY (Crossroad) 1990. For the divine presence in the context of love poems and their religious texture, see Mathieu: *La poésie amoureuse ...*, 1996, pp. 232-41.

[6] The most integrated and complete study of the love poems is the PhD Thesis of Bernard Mathieu: *La poésie amoureuse ...*, 1996, published by *IFAO*; see *op. cit.*, pp. 5-12 for an Egyptological bibliography pertaining to this very issue. Excellent books on the subject of ancient Egyptian love poetry are also the following: Fox: *The Song of Songs ...*, 1985, already cited above (see footnote 1); Hermann, A.: *Altägyptischen Liebesdichtung*, Wiesbaden (O. Harrasso-witz) 1959.; Maravelia, A.-A.: *The Love Poems of Ancient Egypt. Foreword, Introduction, Translation from the Original, Commentaries, Indexes*, Athens (Harmos) 1996; Schott, S.: *Les chants d'amour de l'Égypte Ancienne*, Paris (Maisonneuve) ²1992; Vernus, P.: *Chants d'amour de l'Égypte Antique*, Paris (Imprimerie Nationale) 1992. Fine translations into English of many of those poems can be found in the following books: Lichtheim, M.: *Ancient Egyptian Literature. A Book of Readings*, **II**, Berkeley (University of CA Press) 1976, pp. 179-93; Manniche, L.: *Sexual Life in Ancient Egypt*, London (KPI) 1987, pp. 74-95; Simpson, W.K. (ed., *et al.*): *The Literature of Ancient Egypt. An Anthology of Stories, Instructions and Poetry*, New Haven (Yale University Press) ²1973, pp. 296-326. Another good translation into French can be found in UNESCO: *Textes sacrés et textes profanes de l'ancienne Égypte**. Mythes, contes et poésies* (traductions et commentaires par Lalouette, C.; préface de Grimal, P.), Paris (Gallimard) 1987, pp. 249-66. See also *LÄ*, **III**, 1980, art. "Liebeslieder", cols. 1048-52; and Posener, G. *et al.*: *Dictionnaire de la civilisation Égyptienne*, Paris (Hazan) 1992, pp. 224-5: art. "Poésie Amoureuse". See also Kischewitz, H.: *Liebe Sagen. Lyrik aus dem Ägyptischen Altertum*, Leipzig (P. Reclam) ³1982; and White, J.B.: *A Study of the Language of Love in the Song of Songs and Ancient Egyptian Poetry*, Missoula (Scholar's Press, *Society of Biblical Literature Dissertation Series*, **38**) 1978 Finally, cf. Wrezinski, W.: *Von Altägyptischen Lyric*, Grenzland 1922.

Beds; II.7. Floral Love Symbols and Diadems of Flowers; II.8. The Mother of the Bride; II.9. The Latent Osiris/Adonis Myth; II.10. The Altar/Table of Offerings; II.11. The Aroma of Incense as an Erotic/Metaphysical Symbol; II.12. The *Paraklausithyra*/Visiting the Lover's Home. Those cases will be re-examined and extended in the following Section II, while their classification will be summarized in a comparative table.

II. Comparative study of the poems

In this paper the rough classification scheme given in the previous one, is revisited, extended and presented anew in Table 1, below. Table 1 has been compiled after all the Sapphic fragments (S) and more than 95% of the extant Love Poems of ancient Egypt (LP) have been extensively studied and thoroughly checked[7]. Table 1 quotes all the passages from Sapphic fragments (S) and Egyptian Love Poems (LP), presenting common poetic themes. Those passages are divided in 13 categories (II^D:1-13), comprising direct/well correlated common themes, and 2 more categories (II^I: 14-15), either comprising indirect/poorly correlated, or well correlated but with a text other than LP. Three asterisks denote excellent correlation; two a very good one; a single a good one; no asterisk means poor correlation. It is to be noted that not all the Sapphic fragments are well correlated to their corresponding LP passages. This table does not include all references to Aphrodite mainly the indirect ones, and Adonis found in S.

Most of those categories were discussed and examined in the previous paper [Maravelia, 2001]. The new classification scheme (cf. Table 1) comprises the following categories: 1. Aphrodite/Hathor; 2. Wreaths of Flowers and Sensual Gardens; 3. A Lonely Lady in Nocturnal Arousal; 4. The Prettiest Star/Sothis; 5. The Mother of the Bride; 6. Palpitating Heart; 7. The Issue of Abandonment; 8. Luxurious Beds and Clothes; 9. Altars and Incense; 10. Dawn and the Shining Earth; 11. A Nocturnal Invocation to a Deity; 12. Visiting the Lover's Home/*Paraklausithyra*; and 13. The Lover as Demigod versus Prince Mehy. Two additional categories of either indirect/very poorly correlated or well correlated, but with a text other than LP are presented here, namely: 14. The latent Osiris/Adonis Myth; and 15. A Common Poetical Wisdom Locus from Sappho and the *Teachings of Ptahhotep*. Here, these cases will be shortly re-discussed and the new categories (10, 11 & 13) will be dealt with in more detail.

1. *Aphrodite/Hathor*: This very theme, presumably the most important and frequent in both texts, has been thoroughly discussed in the former paper [Maravelia, 2001: § II.1], where the cross identification of the two goddesses in both S and LP was pointed out[8]. It will suffice to state that all the references to both goddesses have been extensively studied here, and were correlated if this was possible. The correlation in Table 1, II^D.1: 1, 11 is the most striking (see also Figure 1). In the first instance the goddess is praised and exalted; in the second instance the priestess of the goddess is highly admired. The correlation in II^D.1: 2 is not so strong, but the evident similarity between Aphrodite's invocation to pour divine wine, and the offering of mandrake wine to god Ptah should be noted[9]. In II^D.1: 3, Sappho is begging the goddess to offer her a good lot in love; this is very well correlated with three instances from the LP, where the Golden goddess is asked to bring the lady to her beloved man as an offering, & c. In II^D.1: 5, 14 the correlation is not so strong, but there is a certain similarity; especially in the second instance, where the common theme of intoxication by love and beverages is mentioned. No direct or well-established correlation was detected in the remainder instances II^D.1: 4, 6, 7, 8, 9, 10, 12 & 13.

2. *Wreaths of flowers and sensual gardens*: This is another relatively very frequent issue, which was already discussed in the previous paper, together with the significance of the floral diadems [Maravelia, 2001: § II.7]. It will suffice to state that all the references to those lovely symbols have been extensively studied here, and were correlated in all instances. The correlation in II^D.2: 2, 3 & 4 is very good; those in II^D.2: 1, 5 & 6 are less strong, although evident. In II^D.2: 2, some of the most sensual flowers of the Greek and Egyptian flora are mentioned with admiration; while in

---

[7] The most fragmentary and/or uncertain love poems are those found in the following sources: *pAnastasi II*, *pDeM 43*, *oErmitage 1125*, *oMichaelides 55* & *86*, *oDeM 1657*, *oDeM1716*, *oDeM1733* & *oCGTurin57544*; for those see Mathieu: *La poésie amoureuse* ..., 1996, pp. 115-9, passim. Some other, less fragmentary sources are: *oDeM1038*, *oDeM1040*, *oDeM1078 r+v*, *oDeM 1079*, *oDeM1636*, *oDeM1646-48*, *oDeM1650-53*, *oLeipzig 6*, and *oCG25761*; for those see Maravelia: *The Love Poems* ..., 1996, pp. 147-54, 223-8, passim; see also Mathieu: *La poésie amoureuse* ..., 1996, pp. 19-22, 115-9, passim. For the LP which do not contain common points with S, see the footnote of Table 2.

[8] In the *Homeric hymns* to her (*V*: l. 1, *VI*: l. 1), as well as in Hesiodos (*Erga kai hêmerai*: ll. 65, 521; *Theogonia*: ll. 822, 962, 1005, 1014; & c.), and in Theokritos (*XV Eidyllion*, l. 101) Aphrodite is either characterised by a composite epithet containing "–golden", or is related to gold. It is to be noted that in the *Orphic hymns*, there is one dedicated to the goddess; at a certain point (*LV*, ll. 18-9), she is described as "lady of the fecund baths of the Egyptian valleys, where chariots wrought in gold are running". For the close relation and piety of Sappho towards Aphrodite see Weigall: *Sappho of Lesbos* ..., ²1937, chapter XVI: "Sappho's Invocation to Aphrodite". The rather common ladies' title "priestess of Hathor" was in use since the OK; see for instance Fischer, H.G.: *Egyptian Women of the Old King-dom and of the Heracleopolitan Period*, NY (The Metropolitan Museum of Art) 1989, p. 12.

[9] Ptah is the god "beautiful–of–countenance", for whom cf. also footnote 19, below. For mandrake, known as *mandragora officinalis* (*rrmt*), persea–trea and lotus–flowers, in the context of the ancient Egyptian love poems, see Derchain, P.: "Le lotus, la mandragore et le perséa", *CdE*, **L/99**, 1975, pp. 65-86.

Table 1: Quotation of passages from Sapphic fragments (S, from *LG* = *Lyra Graeca*) and Egyptian Love Poems (LP), presenting common poetic themes. They are divided in 13 categories (II^D: 1-13), comprising direct/well correlated common themes, and 2 more categories (II^I: 14-15), either comprising indirect/very poorly correlated themes or well correlated ones, but with a text other than LP. Three asterisks denote excellent correlation; two, a very good one; a single, a good one; no asterisk means poor correlation. Not all Sapphic fragments are well correlated to the corresponding LP passages. This table does not include all references to Aphrodite and Adonis in S.

1. Aphrodite/Hathor.
1. ***LG*, 1, ll. 1-2 & 8-9: ποικιλόθρον' ἀθάνατ' Ἀφρόδιτα, παῖ Δίος δολόπλοκε, λίσσομαί σε ... ... χρύσιον ἦλθες ἄρμ' ὑπασδεύξαισα· ***pChester Beatty I, v, C3, ll. 4-5: dw3w.i Nbwt ... sk3y.i nbt pt iry.i i3wt n Ḥwt-Ḥr 2. *LG*, 6, ll. 1-4:] ἔλθε Κύπρι χρυσίαισιν ἐν κυλίκεσσιν ἄβρως συμμεμιγμένον θαλίαισι νέκταρ οἰνοχόεισα *pHarris 500, r, II, l. 9: Mn-Nfr g3y n rrmwt w3ḥ.ti m-b3ḥ Nfr-Ḥr 3. **LG*, 9, ll. 1-2: αἴ θ' ἔγω χρυσοστέφαν' Ἀφρόδιτα, τόνδε τὸν πάλον λαχόην **pChester Beatty I, r, 17, l. 1: m Nbwt iwḏ.st n.k m f3yt & **pChester Beatty I, v, C2, l. 3: tw.i wḏ.kwi ḥr.k in Nbwt ḥmwt & *pChester Beatty I, v, G2, l. 5: in Nbwt wḏ s[t] n.k 4. *LG*, 37, l. 1: [Κύ]πρι, κα[ί σ]ε πι[κροτέρ]αν ἐπεῦρ[εν. 5. *LG*, 45, ll. 7-11: ... τ[όδ]ε μέμφ[εταί σοι] [Κ]υπρογέν[ηα], [τ]ᾶς ἄραμα[ι τοῦτο τω[[β]όλλομα[ι *pChester Beatty I, v, C4, ll. 3-4: Nbwt h3y im sw m ib.st

6. *LG*, 156 & 158, l. 3:
...] τετίμακ' ἔξοχά σ' Ἀφρόδιτα.

7. *LG*, 125-6, l. 2:
... τί τὰν πολύολβον Ἀφροδίταν;

8. *LG*, 123:
ζά ... ἐλεξάμαν ὄναρ Κυπρογένηα

9. *LG*, 134:
δολοπλόκας γὰρ Κυπρογένεος πρόπολον

10. *Lobel*, I.A. 19:
πτέρα δ' ἄγνα πὰρ Ἔρωτος Ἀφροδίτα

11. ***LG, 24:
χρυσοφάην θερ[άπαιν]αν Ἀφροδίτ[ας

***sLouvre C100, l. 1:
bnr bnr mrwt Mwt-irt-di.s ḥmt-nṯr Ḥwt-Ḥr

12. *LG*, 157, ll. 1-2:
ὦ καλ', ὦ χαρίεσσα, σοι αἱ βροδόσφυροι Χάριτες
Χρύσια τ' Ἀφρόδιτα συμπαίζοισι

[cf. also Theokritos' *XV Eidyllion*, l. 101:
... χρυσῷ παίζοισ' Ἀφροδίτα, ...]

13. *LG*, 33:
ὦ γένος θελξίβροτον Ἀφροδίτας

14. *LG, 86A, APP., ll. 6-8:
... καὶ δαμ[ασσικάρδι]ος Ἀφρόδιτα,
κὰδ δὲ μ[έλλιχον νέκταρ ἔχευ' ἀπὺ
χρυσίας [φρενω]λοία ...

**pChester Beatty I*, r, 16, l. 10:
ʿpr.st m ḥswt ḫbw irpw ḏsrw <m> šwt.st

15. *LG*, 147, ll. 1-2:
[νύμφα ῥοδέων ἐρώτων βρύουσα,
νύμφα Παφίης ἄγαλμα κάλλιστον, ...]

2. Wreaths of Flowers (*m3ḥw*) & Sensual Gardens.

1. **LG*, 117, ll. 1-4:
σὺ δὲ στεφάνοις, ὦ Δίκα, πέρθεσθ' ἐράταις φόβαισιν
ὄρπακας ἀνήτω συναέρραισ' ἀπάλαισι χέρσιν·
εὐάνθεα γὰρ πέλεται καὶ Χάριτες μάκαιραι
μᾶλλον προσόρην· ἀστεφανώτοισι δ' ἀπυστρέφονται

*oGardiner 304, r, ll. 2-4:
iw n3y.st šbyw n ḥrrwt n3[y.st krmwt] n isw
... iw p3y.st sšn m ḏ(r)t.st

2. ***LG*, 83, ll. 13-8:
π[όλλοις γὰρ στεφά]νοις ἴων καὶ βρ[όδων κρο]κίων τ' ὔμοι
κἀν [ ] παρ' ἔμοι παρεθήκαο, καὶ πό[λλαις ὐπα]θύμιδας
πλέκ[ταις ἀνπ' ἀπ]άλαι δέραι ἀνθέων ἐ[ράτων] πεποημμέναις ...

**oDeM 1266 + oCG25218, ll. 22-24:
ḫ3nr.n.i snt m-mnt mi w3ḏw3ḏ m3ḥw
[mi n3] isw šwy(w) p3 k3ṯ3 prḥw mrbbw
<m> ḥnw p3 ḥsbd n3 rrmwt ...

3. ***LG*, 86, ll. 12-4:
... ἀ δ' ἐέρσα κάλα κέχυται τεθάλαισι δὲ βρόδα
κἄπαλ' ἄνθρυσκα καὶ μελίλωτος ἀνθεμώδης·

**pTurin 1966, r, I, l. 8:
m sšnw prḥw [...] m nḥmw

4. ***LG*, 67:
αὐτάορα ἐστεφαναπλόκην

**oDeM 1079 + oGardiner 339, l. 3:
... st ḥr ṯ3[t] ḥrrwt ...

5. **LG*, 82, ll. 9-10:
... ἄνθινοι στέφανοι περ[ὶ σὸν κάρα] δέθεντες, ...

*oDeM 1266 + oCG25218, l. 24:
iw.st m di.i m-mnt mi w3ḏw3ḏ m3ḥw ḥrrwt nbt

6. **LG*, 64:
στεφάνοισι σελιννίνοις

*pHarris 500, r, VII, ll. 11-12:
ṯ(3)tw im.f ṯ3y.i n3y.k m3ḥw iw.k ii.ti tḫ.<t>w

3. A Lonely Lady in Nocturnal Arousal.

***LG, 111, ll. 1-2:
δέδυκε μὲν ἀ σέλαννα καὶ Πληΐαδες, μέσαι δὲ νύκτες,
παρὰ δ᾽ ἔρχετ᾽ ὥρα, ἔγω δὲ μόνα κατεύδω

***oDeM 1266 + oCG25218, l. 1:
mrwt.k m hrw grḥ wnwt sḏr.kwi rs.kwi r ḥḏ t3

4. The Prettiest Star/Sothis.

***LG, 32:
ἀστέρων πάντων ὁ κάλλιστος

***pChester Beatty I, v, C1, ll. 1-2:
ptri.st mi Spdt ḫꜥy m ḥ3t rnpt nfrt sšpt iḳrt

5. The Mother of the Bride.

**LG, 135, ll. 1-2:
γλύκηα μᾶτερ, οὔτοι δύναμαι κρέκην τὸν ἴστον
πόθωι δάμεισα παῖδος βραδίναν δι᾽ Ἀφροδίταν

**pHarris 500, r, IV, ll. 8-9:
iḫ k3.i n m(w)t.i šmt(.i) r.s tnw hrw iw.i 3tp.kwi m gry
bw grg.i (m) pḫ3 m p3 hrw iṯ{t}.wi mrwt.k

6. Palpitating Heart.

**LG, 2, ll. 5-16:
... τὸ μ᾽ ἦ μὰν καρδίαν ἐν στήθεσιν ἐπτόαισεν·
ὡς γὰρ ἐς σ᾽ ἴδω βρόχε᾽ ὥς με φώναισ᾽ οὐδ᾽ ἒν ἔτ᾽ εἴκει,
ἀλλὰ κὰμ μὲν γλῶσσα Ϝέαγε,
λέπτον δ᾽ αὔτικα χρῶι πῦρ ὑπαδεδρόμακεν,
ὀππάτεσι δ᾽ οὐδ᾽ ἒν ὄρρημμ᾽, ἐπιρρόμβεισι δ᾽ ἄκουαι,
ἀ δὲ μ᾽ ἴδρως κακχέεται, τρόμος δὲ παῖσαν ἄγρει,
χλωροτέρα δὲ ποίας ἔμμι, τεθνάκην δ᾽ ὀλίγω 'πιδεύην φαίνομ᾽...

**pChester Beatty I, v, C2, ll. 9-10:*
ifd(w) sw ib.i 3s dr sh3.i mrwt.k
bw dd.f šm.i mi rmṯ sw tfy <m> mkt.f

&

**pChester Beatty I, v, C4, l. 5:*
... tf ib.i r pr(t) ...

&

**pChester Beatty I, v, C4, l. 7:*
ꜥkꜥk.n.i h3yt im.i hpr.kwi hꜥwt.i wdnw
shm(.i) dt.i ds.i

&

**pChester Beatty I, v, G2, l. 2:*
rdwy.f(y) (hr) šm hꜥwt.f (hr) ghy hryt ꜥk.ti m hꜥwt.f

7. The Issue of Abandonment.

***LG, 22 & 124, ll. 1-3:*
] ἦ τιν' ἄλλον μᾶλλον ἀνθρώπων ἔμεθεν φίλησθα;
ἔμεθεν δ' ἔχηισθα λάθαν;

***pHarris 500, r, V, ll. 11-12:*
r dd n.i ꜥd3.f wi k3-dd gm.f kt
sw hr gg n hr.f ih rf p3 hd-ib n ky hr hppw

8.   Luxurious Beds and Clothes.

1. **LG, 56:*
ἔγω δ' ἐπὶ μολθάκαν τύλαν κασπολέω μέλεα

**pChester Beatty I, r, 17, ll. 12-13:*
gm.f hꜥti nmꜥw m p3kt šri<t> nfrt r-hnꜥw

2. **LG, 83, ll. 22-3:*
... καὶ στρώμν[αν ἐ]πὶ μολθάκαν ἀπάλαν ...

**oDeM 1266 + oCG25218, l. 17:*
im p3kt r-imytw hꜥwt.st m nmꜥ n.s m sšr-nsw

9.	**Altars (ḫ3wt) & Incense (snṯr).**

1. ***LG, 40, l. 15:
[ἀ]μφί σ[όν βῶμον πύκιναι στάθεισαι]

**pChester Beatty I, r, 17, ll. 4-5:
gm(.n.i) sn m t3 ḫnn rd.f w3ḥ ḥr itrw
sw (ḥr) irt ḫ3wt n(t) wrš(w)

2. *LG, 66, l. 31:
... μύρρα καὶ κασία λίβανός τ' ὀνεμείχνυτο ...

*pHarris 500, r, VII, l. 8:
m ḫ3wt nb(t) nḏm sty

3. LG, 112, ll. 1-2:
πλήρης μὲν ἐφαίνετ' ἀ σελάννα
αἰ δ' ὡς περὶ βῶμον ἐστάθησαν

4. LG, 114, l. 2:
... ὤρχηντ' ἀπάλοισ' ἀμφ' ἐρόεντα βῶμον, ...

5. *Barnstone, 29, ll. 3-4:
... βῶμοι δὲ τεθυμιάμενοι [λι]βανώτωι ...

*oDeM 1266 + oCG25218, l. 4:
mi snṯr{i} r fnd [...] ꜥk.f r [...]
&
*oBorchardt 1 + oCGTurin 57367, v, ll. 2-4:
sšp.tw.st m ḥnḳt ḥr snṯr{i} mi p3 sḥtp nṯr

10.	**Dawn and the Shining Earth.**

1. **LG, 3, ll. 3-4:
... πλήθοισα μάλιστα λάμπησ' ἀργυρία γᾶν

**pHarris 500, r, V, l. 6:
p3 t3 (ḥr) ḥḏ

2. **LG, 94, ll. 2-4:
... ὁπότα φλόγι [ὁ θέ]ος κατέτα [γάα]ν
ἐπι[πε]πτάμενος καταύγη

**pHarris 500, r, II, ll. 8-9:
ḥḏ t3 m nfrw.st

11. A Nocturnal Invocation to a Deity.

***LG, 36, ll. 17-20:
... [ἀλλ' ἄκουσον]ον, αἴ κ[ε, θέα, μέλεσ]σι [σοὶ φρέν ἰαινο]ν,
σὺ [δὲ] λύγ[ρ' ἐ]ρέ[μ]ναι [νύκτι πάντα κατ]θεμ[έ]να κάκαν
[παρ'] [ἄμμιν ἀλάλκο]ις

***oDeM 1266 + oCG25218, ll. 26-27:
sw3š.i sw m nfrw grḥ ... [...] ... ḏwt nbt m ḥʿt[.i]

12. Visiting the Lover's Home / *Paraklausithyra*.

**LG, 46, ll. 1-2:
... καὶ γὰρ δὴ σύ [μ' ἴες] προτ[' οἶκον]
[ἄρτ]ι κἤσμελπες κ[ατὰ] ταῦτα [δ' ἤκω.] ...

**pChester Beatty I, v, C3, l. 10:
sw3.n<.i> m-h3w n pr.f gm(.n).i ʿ3.f wn
&
**pChester Beatty I, r, 17, ll. 7-8:
sn<.i> pr.st wḫ3t {k} thm.i bw wn n.i

13. The Lover as Demigod versus Prince Mehy.

**LG, 2, ll. 1-2:
φαίνεταί μοι κῆνος ἴσος θέοισιν ἔμμεν' ὤνηρ, ...

*oDeM 1078, v, l. 4:
w3ḥ.n m-b3ḥ Mḥ[y]
&
**pHarris 500, r, V, l. 4:
m n3 <n> nhwt [w3y r.i p3]y.i ʿ3 m p3 grḥ

14.   The Latent Osiris/Adonis Myth.
LG, 103, ll. 1-2: κατθναίσκει, Κυθέρη᾽, ἄβρος Ἄδωνις τί κε θεῖμεν; καττύπτεσθε, κόραι, καὶ κατερείκεσθε χίτωνας *oNash 12*, r, l. 4: ḥnʿ nty m t3 ḏrit (m) pḫ3 (m) pt rʿ nb & *pHarris 500*, r, V, ll. 4-5: tw.i mi nty m p3y.i (i)s
15. A Similar Poetical Wisdom Locus from Sappho and the *Teachings of Ptahhotep*.
***LG, 38, ll. 21-2: [εὖ μὲν ἴδ]μεν οὐ δύνατον γένεσθαι [λῷστ'] ὀν᾽ ἀνθρώπ[οις, π]εδέχην δ᾽ ἀρασθαι ***pPrisse, 5, ll. 9-10: n in.tw ḏrw ḥmt nn ḥmww ʿpr 3ḥw.f

II^D.2: 3, the beauty of a perfumed prairie is described in a most irresistible manner. Finally, in II^D.2: 4, a tiny fragment of S hints to one of a similar verse from a fragmentary LP ostracon: the beloved cute young girl is collecting flowers in a sensual garden of delights[10]. For a banqueting scene with flowers and floral offerings see Figure 2.

3. *A lonely lady in nocturnal arousal*: This issue has also been discussed in the previous paper [Maravelia, 2001: § II.2], and is one of the most striking common points between the texts of S and LP, as can be seen from Table 1, II^D.3. In both instances, the apparent diurnal rotation of the celestial sphere, creating the alternation of night and day, consists the scenery/background, which counts the psychological time of loneliness for the young woman, who desperately desires her mate[11].

4. *The prettiest star/Sothis*: Another interesting similar theme, which was already discussed in the former paper [Maravelia, 2001: § II.3], is reexamined here. As is evident, from the comparison of both texts in S and LP (cf. Table 1, II^D.4), the resemblance is striking. It will suffice to notice here that while the Egyptian text mentions Sirius[12],

---

[10] For the flora of Mytilênê, see Cantargy, P.C.: "Flore de l'île de Lesbos", *Bull. Soc. Bot. de France*, **45**, 1898. For "melilôtos", see Taylor, W.: *Flowers of Greece and the Aegean*, London 1977, pp. 300-1: art. "Melilotus", where more can be found about all the flowers mentioned. For the ancient Egyptian flora, see Germer, R.: *Flora des Pharaonischem Ägypten*, Mainz 1985. See also Manniche, L.: *An Ancient Egyptian Herbal*, London (BMP) 1989; and Manniche, L.: *Egyptian Luxuries: Fragrance, Aromatherapy, and Cosmetics in Pharaonic Times*, Cairo (The AUC Press) 1999, chapters 1, 5 & 6, passim. For "*t3t*" flowers see Mathieu: *La poésie amoureuse ...*, 1996, p. 80, footnote 260. On the topic of a terrestrial paradise of love see Chabas, F.: "The Tale of the Garden of Flowers", *Records of the Past*, **VI**, 1876, pp. 151-6; cf. also the old novel by Sheikh 'al-Nafzawi: *'al-raūd 'al-'atīr, fī nuzHat 'al-Hatīr* [*La prairie parfumée, où s'ébattent les plaisirs*, Paris (Phébus) 1984], whose title and erotic content alludes to the texts under study in this paper.

[11] Night as a goddess is praised in an ancient Greek charming hymn (*Orphic Hymns*: 3). Night, as the *creatrix* of everything, is assimilated to Aphrodite(/Hathor) in this context, although no other direct or indirect reference to any love affair is mentioned. In l. 10 of this hymn it is said that night "brings light to the depths (of the world)", hence alluding to a presumably common Egyptian belief, that the "nocturnal sun" illuminates the Underworld realms.

[12] See for instance, *LÄ*, **V**, 1984, cols. 1110-17: art. "Sothis". Apart from the sun and the moon, only Sothis (*Spdt*), corresponding to α–Canis Majoris (aka Sirius), the brightest star of the sky, acquired a cult as the herald of the river's inundation. From the early Dynastic period onwards she was worshipped in the form of a cow, but was soon perceived to be a

the extant Greek text doesn't mention explicitly any specific star or planet; while, in another Sapphic fragment (*LG*, 149, 1. 1) Hesperos (bringer of children to their mothers upon dusk) is mentioned, which was identified to planet Venus[13]. Venus was considered by the Egyptians as a planet closely related to Osiris, and his sacred *phoenix* bird (*bnw*). For a related representation of Sothis, see Figure 3.

5. *The mother of the bride*: This issue has been already dealt with in the previous paper [Maravelia, 2001: § II.8]. It should be noted here that the text from S belongs also to the first category $II^D.1$, because a reference to Aphrodite is met, while in LP there is no reference to Hathor. In S (cf. Table 1, $II^D.5$) the young girl can not continue weaving, while in LP she is wondering what to tell her mother, for she didn't put bird-traps; both of them having lost their minds due to their love for a youth[14].

6. *Palpitating heart*: This theme was also discussed in the previous paper [Maravelia, 2001: § II.4]. The description of love–panic, palpitating hearts and love–illness in both S and LP is excellent, especially in the first, third and fourth instances in LP (cf. Table 1, $II^D.6$). The likening of the lady–love to a gazelle[15] in the last instance is very lyrical and creates a natural scenery for the evolution of the poem.

7. *The issue of abandonment*: This case (cf. Table 1, $II^D.7$) has been already discussed in the previous paper [Maravelia, 2001: § II.5]. There is an evident similarity in the descriptive mode of both passages from S and LP, which is certainly appealing. The correlation of both texts seems to be excellent indeed, alluding to the expression of simple and daily issues in such a sincere poetic manner[16].

8. *Luxurious beds and clothes*: This issue has been already dealt with in the previous paper [Maravelia, 2001: § II.6]. Here another new similar instance from LP is given (cf. Table 1, $II^D.8$, 1), describing the sensual luxury of well-prepared beds, covered by fine linen sheets. The lover is wishing to find his girl friend, lying in such a bed and waiting for him to join her[17].

9. *Altars and incense*: Those two cases have already been examined in the previous paper [Maravelia, 2001: §§ II.10-11]. Here they are grouped under the same category, which is enriched by more instances from both S and LP (cf. Table 1, $II^D.9$: 1-5). It is to be noted that in S the altar ritual is performed by night, especially when the moon is full; while in LP the mention of the morning feast/altar is just once met[18]. The correlation here is not so strong and not evident in all instances.

---

manifestation of Isis, just as Osiris was identified to Orion (*S3h*). Along with her husband and her son (*Spd*), she belonged to a Triad which paralleled that of Osiris/Isis/Horus. For Sothis cf. also Vandier, J.: *Manuel d'archéologie égyptienne*, **1**, Paris 1952, pp. 842-3; see also Kákosy, L.: "Die Mannweibliche Natur des Sirius in Ägypten", *Studia Aegyptiaca*, **2**, Budapest 1976, pp. 41-6. For a depiction of Sothis as an astral cow, cf. also Figure 3.

[13] Venus is an "inner" planet, and because of its close proximity to the sun (which is although lesser than that of Mercury) its visibility occurs either just after sunset, or just before dawn. Venus was called by ancient Egyptians (*sb3*) *d3 Bnw Wsir*, and was the planet most closely connected to Osiris and its cult. On this topic see for instance, Neugebauer, O. & Parker, R.A.: *Egyptian Astronomical Texts*, *III: Decans, Planets, Constellations and Zodiacs*, RI (Brown University Press) 1969, pp. 180-2; see also Maravelia, A.–A.: "On Astronomy in Ancient Egypt", *Platôn*, **49**, 1997, pp. 207–35. In ancient Greece it was called *Hesperos*, when visible just after sunset, due to its apparent "proximity" to the West; when visible just before sunrise, it was called *Eôsphoros*, literally "bringer of dawn". For the planets, see also Neugebauer, O.: "Egyptian Planetary Texts", *Transactions of the American Philoso-phical Society*, **XXXII**^{2} (new series), 1942, pp. 209-50 (& plates).

[14] This is a clever metaphor, assimilating the capture by traps to love captivity. For a bird–trapping picture see *oBruxelles E.6769*, in Mathieu: *La poésie amoureuse ...*, 1996, p. 68: fig. 3. For more depictions of bird hunting inside marshes see also Shedid, A.G. & Seidel, M: *Das Grab des Nacht*, Mainz (P. von Zabern) 1991, pp. 56-7, 58-9, 60-2, 65, 66-7, 71, 72, where such scenes from the tomb of Nakht (Th.T. 52) are presented. A brief comparison of the role both deities were playing in love affairs has to be given here. Aphrodite was thought to intervene more like a human female, sometimes jealous, sometimes with ardent passion, in order not only to help mortals in their love quests, but also to perplex situations and punish them (cf. the text from S in Table 1, $II^D.1$: 4, 5, 9 & $II^D.5$). Hathor, on the contrary, intervenes more like a benevolent *dea ex machina*, just to help the lovers, or offer one to the other miraculously, thus never putting them in trouble or love torments (cf. the text from LP in Table 1, $II^D.1$: 1, 3, 11, 14). It is to be noted that while Sappho compares with a considerable ease the beauty of a cute lady to the divine beauty of Aphrodite (cf. the text from S in Table 1, $II^D.1$: 6, 12, 13, 15), this is never the case in the LP text. In the LP, with the exception of $II^D.4$ (where the lady–love is compared to the stellar goddess Sothis), there is no other explicit or direct comparison between a mortal woman and a goddess. This hints to the fact that ancient Greek divinities were conceived more as projections of humans and their souls and passions (as well as manifestations of natural phenomena), than was the case in ancient Egypt. On this topic see Hornung, E.: *Conceptions of God in Ancient Egypt. The One and the Many* (translated by Baines, J.), NY (Cornell University Press) ^{2}1996, pp. 256: "Egypt differs markedly from Greece, where both the temples and the gods are relatively finished and complete. However much information we assemble about Egyptian gods, and however receptive we become to their reality, we will never be able to see them as the clear figures that Walter F. Otto perceived in the gods of Greece". Cf. also the reference to Mathieu at the end of footnote 5, above.

[15] In both passages from S and LP the descriptive power is irresistible. The most touching instance is the fourth from the LP (the others describe the issue of love panic, using every day terms), where the anxiety of love embarrassment is described with a metaphor, borrowed from the Egyptian fauna. For the ancient Egyptians the gazelle (*oryx gazella*) was presumably symbolising not only speed, but sensitivity and grace as well. For this topic see *LÄ*, **I**, 1975, cols. 319-23: art. "Antilope" & *LÄ*, **II**, 1977, cols. 426-7: art. "Gazelle". Hunting antelopes was a common royal and noble's sport, for which see Decker, W.: *Sports and Games in Ancient Egypt* (Guttmann, A., transl.), New Haven 1992, pp. 147-67.

[16] For the difficulties and bitter face of love see Venus: *Chants d'amour ...*, 1992, pp. 32-38, & p. 36 for this very verse. The love disappointments of Sappho were also real and her inner solitude was probably tormenting her, although her life must have been generally speaking "busy". Cf. for instance Weigall: *Sappho of Lesbos ...*, ^{2}1937, chapters IX: "Sappho and her Hetaerae" & XIV: "Sappho at Home".

[17] Fine (royal) linen (*p3kt, sšr-nsw*) was highly esteemed in ancient Egypt as a luxury product and is referred to in the LP as bestowing a sensual undertone. Concerning linen see Posener, G. et al.: *Dictionnaire ...*, 1992, pp. 149–150: art. "Lin".

[18] Both in ancient Egypt and Greece, altars were used to carry offerings intended to propitiate the deities. On this topic see for instance Jéquier, G.: "Autel", *BIFAO*, **19**, 1922, pp. 236-49. Accordingly, the incense was used for a bloodless sacrifice, as is the custom borrowed from the old ways even today. For this topic see Blackman, A.M.: "The Significance of Incense and Libations in Funerary and Temple Rituals", *ZÄS*, **50**,

10. *Dawn and the shining earth*: This is a case not examined in the previous paper. Here (cf. Table 1, II^D.10: 1, 2) two instances from S and LP are presented, which are well correlated. In the first one, the way of expression in S (meaning literally brightening of the earth, by the silver rays of the full moon) is similar in that from LP, where the same expression denotes the dawn. In the second one, a flying divinity brightens the earth with flame in S, while in LP the world shines by the beauty of love, a shining presumably created by the divine intervention of Ptah, Sekhmet, Nefertem and Iadyt. The use of the same hieroglyphic sign (Gardiner's taxogram T3) to denote "silver", "white", "bright" and "dawn" is to be noted[19].

11. *A nocturnal invocation to a deity*: This is another instance not examined in the previous paper. The correlation is excellent and the similarity of those poetical loci is striking (cf. Table 1, II^D.11), since in both S and LP, the invocation to dispel evil is performed either in the midst of the night, or it is asked that all negativity be trapped by the blackness of the night. It is to be noted, that while in S Sappho is praying for her brother, in LP the lover is praying for her beloved lady, asking that she might join him for ever, in a kind of love–magic spell[20].

12. *Visiting the lover's home/Paraklausithyra*: This case has also been dealt with in the previous paper [Maravelia, 2001: § II.12]. It is to be noted here that the first LP text (cf. Table 1, II^D.12) refers to the visit of the young lady to her lover's home, where she finds his family waiting for her; in this context it is more closely related to the text from S. The second text form the LP reminds a *Paraklausithyron*: here the man is visiting by night the home of her beloved lady, but the door of the house is found closed[21].

13. *The lover as demigod versus prince Mehy*: This is another instance not examined in the previous paper. The correlation of S with the second text from LP is very good, while the correlation with the first text from LP is not so strong. Sappho extols the beauty and courtesan manners of the young man towards his bride in S, assimilating him to a demigod; while in the second (well correlated) LP text the young lady is waiting for her "prince" or "great–one" to come tonight. This "great–one" might be Mehy, the legendary personality met in some instances in LP, who might be a demigod of the Cupidon type; either king Amenophis II who was presenting himself as proud of his physical fitness; or a beautiful military officer of the early XIX Dynasty. In any case, the name Mehy is written inside a royal cartouche in the concomitant case of the first LP text, in which (cf. Table 1, II^D.13), it is followed by the kingship/divinity hieroglyphic sign (Gardiner's G7). In this instance Mehy is addressed as a deity, and praised with offerings[22].

14. *The latent Osiris/Adonis myth*: As it has been already stated in the previous paper [Maravelia, 2001: § II.9], there is an indirect, although related interconnection between Osiris and Adonis (cf. Table 1, II^I.14). The indirect mention of Isis in the first text from the LP, as a kite coming from the sky, was discussed. In this paper another indirect instance is given, where the young lady waiting for her lover, states that she will be like a dead inside the tomb, as soon as she does not meet her man[23].

1912. See also Lucas, A.: *Ancient Egyptian Materials and Industries* (Harris, J.R., rev. ed.), London ^{4}1962, pp. 80-97.

[19] See for instance, Shaw, I. & Nicholson, P.: *British Museum Dictionary of Ancient Egypt*, Cairo (The *AUC* Press) 1996, pp. 230-1: art. "Ptah"; p. 257: art. "Sekhmet"; p. 199: art. "Nefertem". For Sekhmet see also *LÄ*, V, 1984, cols. 323-33: art. "Sachmet". For Nefertem see also *LÄ*, IV, 1982, cols. 378-80: art. "Nefertem". For Ptah see also *LÄ*, IV, 1982, cols. 1177-80: art. "Ptah". For the various references to hieroglyphs in the present article, see Gardiner, A.H.: *Egyptian Grammar. Being an Introduction to the Study of Hieroglyphs*, Oxford (Griffith Institute, Ashmolean Museum) ^{3}1988, pp. 438-548.

[20] As already pointed out in footnote 4, Sappho was praying to Aphrodite, in order that her brother quits Rhodopis. The Egyptian man in the LP instance is invoking the spirit (*k3*) of his god to help him approach his lady–love, a situation which reminds the practice of magic in ancient Egypt. For this topic, concerning the area where most of the LP were found, see Borghouts, J.: "Magical Practices among the Villagers", *Pharaoh's Workers: the Villagers of Deir 'el-Medineh* (Lesko, L.H., ed.), Ithaka & London 1994, pp. 119-30. For some uses of magick in the life of the inhabitants at Deir 'el-Medineh (from the original sources), see also MacDowell, A.G.: *Village Life in Ancient Egypt. Laundry Lists and Love Songs*, UK (Oxford University Press) 1999, pp. 115-7: "Magic"; cf. also pp. 152-7: "Love Songs". See also Pinch, G.: *Magic in Ancient Egypt*, London 1994; and Ritner, R.K.: *The Mechaniccs of Ancient Egyptian Magical Practice*, Chicago 1993.

[21] Actually the provenance of the (re)copied text of this very poem of S is from Egypt (*pOxyrhynchi*, 1231, l. 50 ff). For *Paraklausithyra* it is to be noted that this composite word is derived by "παρα–" (= near) + "κλαίειν" (= to cry) + "θύρα" (= door). Because the man was left outside his desired woman's house, by her on purpose, crying near her door. For this topic in the Egyptian love poems see Hermann: *Liebesdichtung*, 1959, pp. 132-5.

[22] For Mehy see Mathieu: *La poésie amoureuse ...*, 1996, pp. 39, footnotes 53, 56; p. 124, footnote 429; pp. 155-6 & footnotes 520-4. See also Vernus: *Chants d'amour ...*, 1992, p. 49, footnote 20 & p. 174, footnote 10. It can not be said with certainty if Mehy was deified, a fact which seems plausible. On the other hand, the demigod appearance of the Greek youth must be understood in a rather different context, denoting probably his beatitude (*mutatis mutandis* comparable to the divine elation) when being near his beloved lady. On the comparison of mortal's feelings to the divine ones see also footnote 14, above.

[23] The lady feels like dead, hence alluding to the realm of *ntyw-im*, ruled by Osiris. In the former instance, the lady–love is assimilated to a kite (*drit*) flying into the sky every day, alluding to Isis as a falcon, and the man is hoping to follow after her and be with her. For Adonis (and his cult as a lover of Aphrodite), see Husain, S.: *The Goddess. Creation, Fertility and Abundance; The Sovereignty of Woman. Myths and Archetypes*, NY (Little, Brown & C°) 1997, pp. 78, 80-1, 103. The Osirian mysteries in Egypt and the Eleusinian mysteries in Greece, closely connected to the cult of Osiris/Adonis/Triptolemos, were both exhibiting the symbol of the seed (= dying son and/or lover), which is buried and then lives again. See for instance, Kérenyi, C.: *Eleusis: Archetypal Image of Mother and Daughter*, London (RKP) 1967, especially pp. 105-74 (for grains cf. pp. 120-30; for a reference to Adonis cf. p. 171); see also Mylonas, G.: *Eleusis and the Eleusinian Mysteries*, NJ (Princeton University Press) 1961, especially pp. 15-6, 61, 276 (for references to Osiris, Isis & c.). For "Osiris beds", filled with alluvial silt and sown with barley seeds, see Wiederman A.: "Osiris végétant", *Le Muséon*, 3, 1903, pp. 111-23; cf. also Raven, M.J.: "Corn–Mummies", *OMRO*, 63, 1982, pp. 7-38. For the cult and mysteries of Osiris, see Griffiths, J.G.: *The Origins of Osiris and his Cult*, Leiden 1980. See, finally, Frazer, J.G.: *Adonis, Attis, Osiris*, I-II, London ^{3}1927. It is to be noted that "Adonis" is a word of purely Chamito-semitic origin (cf.

15. *A common poetical wisdom locus from Sappho and the Teachings of Ptahhotep*: This was already mentioned in the former paper [Maravelia, 2001: § I]. Although it does not belong to the text of the LP (cf. Table 1, II^I.15), the similarity of thought is striking indeed[24].

The above discussion, as well as Table 1 completes the present study of the common poetical loci in both Sapphic fragments and the ancient Egyptian Love Poems. In the next section (conclusions), the main results of this study will be summarized in Table 2.

III. Conclusions

The possible influence of the ancient Egyptian Love Poems on Sappho's lyrics has been made evident so far, from their comparative study. Here, fifteen cases of common poetical loci were detected, the most frequent of which are: the invocation of the golden Aphrodite/Hathor, and the floral diadems and gardens of flowers. Furthermore, there are some striking parallels, which are not frequent, but their similarity is to be noted: the nocturnal arousal of the lonely woman, the best star/Sothis, the "sweet mother" issue, the palpitating heart, & c., are the most prominent.

Table 2 summarizes the present study, presenting the concomitant statistics. Table 2 was deduced using Table 1. Table 2 presents the frequency of occurrence of a given category (II^D: direct correlation; II^I: indirect/very poor correlation or good correlation with a text other than LP) of common themes in Sappho's lyrics (S) and the examined love poems (LP) of ancient Egypt, as is derived from their study, using Table 1, above. Bold italics refer to the numeration of the quoted passages. $\sum$ denotes only the evident well correlated common petical loci, with nearly or closely identical meaning, in both S & LP. Asterisks denote the five most frequent common poetical loci, for which the concomitant percentages are also given. In the first column, the related Egyptian or Sapphic theme is given; in the shaded area of this column the total sum of the well correlated common poetical loci, together with its percentage, is presented. In the second column, the correspondence and the partial frequency of each category of common loci is given. In the third column, the total frequency for each category is calculated, together with the corresponding percentages for the most frequent ones. It is evident that the most frequent categories are II^D.1 (21%) and II^D.2 (21%). Follow II^D.9 (10 %) and II^D.8 (7%), together with II^D.10 (7%).

It is to be noted that these influences - if not only assumed - might constitute the result of Sappho's exchange of ideas with her brother who was visiting Egypt and had a Graeco-Egyptian concubine, as well as with the known poet Alkaios who also stayed in Egypt and was presumably influenced by the Egyptian thought and literature[25]. Furthermore, the free and open mind of Sappho, together

---

Hebrew יָדִין); this word was incorporated into Greek and was used to denote the male archetype of the Cosmos, dying and being reborn afresh every spring. Theokritos, in his mentioned verses:

... χρυσῷ παίζοισ' Ἀφροδίτα,
οἷόν τοι τὸν Ἄδωνιν ἀπ' ἀενάω Ἀχέροντος
μηνὶ δυωδεκάτῳ μαλακαὶ πόδας ἄγαγον Ὧραι, ...

refers to the myth of Adonis too (*XV: Syrakosiai ê Adôniazousai*, ll. 101-3 & passim). The myth of Adonis is archetypically inherent to the human belief for resurrection, as well as the myth of Osiris and Isis (as mentioned by Ploutarchos in his book *De Iside et Osiride*). Both deities were considered as resurrection divinities and symbols. *Myth* is a paradigmatic narrative, by which a community expresses the account of its origins, while *ritual* consists the enactment of myth under a highly structured and ordered situation. It has already been noted that in Egypt ritualistic mysteries were taking place to commemorate the resurrection of Osiris and his sexual activation by Isis in the form of a mighty female falcon (wherefrom Horus was born). On this topic see for instance, Chassinat, E.: *Le mystère d'Osiris au mois de Khoiak*, **I-II**, Le Caire 1966-68; and Lavier, M.C.: "Les mystères d'Osiris à Abydos, d'après les stèles du Moyen Empire et du Nouvel Empire", *Akten München* (Schoske, S., ed.), **III**, 1985, pp. 289-95. For a translation of a similar liturgical text, the copying of which dates from the early Ptolemaic Period (*pBremner–Rhind* = BM nº 10188), cf. Vernus: *Chants d'amour ...*, 1992, pp. 101-19 & 193-9. On the other hand, the (Adonis–cult–related) Eleusinian mysteries, consacrated to Demeter and Persephone/Kore, were taking place in Greece annually in two parts, the *Lesser* and the *Greater Mysteria*, in order to bestow to the *Mystai* the bliss of eternal life, an acquaintance with hereafter, and possibly an ultimate *visio beatifica* for the most advanced ones. For this topic see finally Gadon, E.W.: *The Once and Future Goddess. A Sweeping Visual Chronicle of the Sacred Female and her Reemergence in the Cultural Myhtology of our Time*, SF (Harper) 1989, pp. 154-7. Concerning the myths and archaeological evidence on the issue of goddess(es), see the interesting book by Goodison, L. and Morris, C. (eds.): *Ancient Goddesses. The Myths and the Evidence*, London (BMP) 1998; cf. in this book the article by Hassan F.A.: "The Earliest Goddesses of Egypt. Divine Mothers and Cosmic Bodies", pp. 98-112, where valuable information on the origins of Egyptian goddesses, like Hathor and Isis can be found; see also in the same book, the article by Voyatzis, M.E.: "From Athena to Zeus. An A–Z Guide to the Origins of Greek Goddesses", pp. 133-47.

[24] For the *Teachings of Ptahhotep*, see Žába, Z.: *Les Maxi-mes de Ptahhotep*, Prague (Académie Tchécoslovaque des Sciences) 1956. Cf. also Jéquier, G.: *Le Papyrus Prisse ses Variantes*, Paris 1911. For a good translation see Simpson (ed., *et al.*): *Anthology ...*, pp. 159-76. It is to be noted that although in the context of Ptahhotep's *sb3yt* there is no reference to love affairs (other than in a marital, familial context), the similarity of thought and the underlying philosophical depth and modesty of both passages is striking.

[25] For the possible influence of Egyptian customs and literature and ways of expression on Alkaios' lyrics, see for instance Weigall: *Sappho of Lesbos ...*, ²1937, pp 229-30. For Alkaios' lyrics see for example Page, D.: *Sappho and Alcaeus. An Introduction to the Study of Ancient Lesbian Poetry*, Oxford (Oxford at the Clarendon Press) ⁵1975; and Reinach, T.: *Alcée–Sapphô*, Paris (Les Belles Lettres) 1937. Examining weather there are similar Egyptian influences on Alkaios' lyrics is something which has to be further investigated. This could check the validity of the theory proposed here. For ancient Greece relatively to the Near East and Egypt, with a reference to Sappho, cf. also Mansfield Haywood, R.: *Ancient Greece and the Near East*, London (Vision) ²1968, pp. 297-8.

Table 2: Frequency of occurrence of a given category (II^D: direct correlation; II^I: indirect/very poor correlation, or good correlation with text other than LP) of common themes in Sappho's lyrics (S) and the examined love poems (LP) of ancient Egypt[†], as is derived from their study using Table 1, above. **Bold italics** refer to the numeration of the quoted passages. Σ denotes only the evident well correlated common poetical loci, with nearly or closely identical meaning, in both S & LP. Asterisks denote the five most frequent terms, for which the concomitant percentages are also given.

	Related Egyptian or Sapphic Theme	**Correspondence & Partial Frequency within Compared Texts, as derived from § II**	**Total Frequency**
II^D $\Sigma=27$ 93%	Ḥwt-Ḥr, Nbwt, nbt pt / χρύσια τ' Ἀφρόδιτα	*1.1* xS1, *1.1* xLP1, *1.2* xS1, *1.2* xLP1, *1.3* xS1, *1.3* xLP3, *1.4* xS1, *1.5* xS1, *1.5* xLP1, *1.6* xS1, *1.7* xS1, *1.8* xS1, *1.9* xS1, *1.10* xS1, *1.11* xS1, *1.11* xLP1, *1.12* xS1, *1.13* xS1, *1.14* xS1, *1.14* xLP1, *1.15* xS1	S=15 LP=8 Σ=6*, 21%
	m3ḥw ḥrrwt / ἄνθινοι στέφανοι	*2.1* xS1, *2.1* xLP1, *2.2* xS1, *2.2* xLP1, *2.3* xS1, *2.3* xLP1, *2.4* xS1, *2.4* xLP1, *2.5* xS1, *2.5* xLP1, *2.6* xS1, *2.6* xLP1	S=6 LP=6 Σ=6*, 21%
	Lonely Lady	*3* xS1, *3* xLP1	S=1 LP=1
	Spdt / ἀστέρων ὁ κάλλιστος	*4* xS1, *4* xLP1	S=1 LP=1
	m(w)t.i / γλύκηα μᾶτερ	*5* xS1, *5* xLP1	S=1 LP=1
	ib.i r pr(t) / καρδία	*6* xS1, *6* xLP4	S=1 LP=4
	Abandonment	*7* xS1, *7* xLP1	S=1 LP=1
	Luxurious Beds	*8.1* xS1, *8.1* xLP1, *8.2* xS1, *8.2* xLP1	S=2 LP=2 Σ=2*, 7%
	Altars & Incense	*9.1* xS1, *9.1* xLP1, *9.2* xS1, *9.2* xLP1, *9.3* xS1, *9.4* xS1, *9.5* xS1, *9.5* xLP2	S=5 LP=4 Σ=3*, 10%
	ḥḏ t3 / [γάα]ν καταύγη	*10.1* xS1, *10.1* xLP1, *10.2* xS1, *10.2* xLP1	S=2 LP=2 Σ=2*, 7%
	Nocturnal Invocation	*11* xS1, *11* xLP1	S=1 LP=1
	Visiting Lover's Home	*12* xS1, *12* xLP2	S=1 LP=2
	Lover as Demigod / Prince Mehy	*13* xS1, *13* xLP2	S=1 LP=2
II^I $\Sigma=2$ 7%	Osiris (indirect hints) / Adonis	*14* xS1, *14* xLP2	S=1 LP=2
	Ptahhotep / Sappho	*15* xS1, *15* xpPr1	S=1 pPr=1

[†] Access to some additional (although fragmentary) sources, like *pAnastasi II, pDeM 43, oErmitage 1125, oMichaelides 55 & 86, oDeM 1657, oDeM1716, oDeM1733 & oCGTurin57544*, was impossible. It is to be noted that some LP sources, like *oDeM1038, oDeM1040, oDeM1636, oDeM1646-48, oDeM1650-53, oLeipzig 6*, and *oCG25761*, do not show any common elements with S.

with her bisexuality must have played an important role[26] – together with her abhorrence towards tyranny[27] – in adopting a certain way of thought that assimilated some influences from the matrifocally structured ancient Egyptian society[28]. Both milieux, that of Sappho's lyrics and that of Egyptian love songs, were noble and courtesan, and this very fact is another interesting element to be taken into account[29].

The case of the previous assumed interaction is characteristic of the general trends in the Mediterranean world of that era, and constitutes a fine paradigm of cultural influence between two civilizations. Should this is true and beyond any doubt might become more evident by the meticulous comparative study of Alkaios' lyrics and Egyptian texts, as well as by the study of the work of various other Graeco-Egyptian poets of the Ptolemaic Era (Theokritos, Kallimachos, *et al.*), who were related to Egypt. The *terminus post quem* for the ancient Egyptian lyrics (with the exception of *sLouvre C100*, which dates from a later period) is c. 1300 BCE, hence the earlier of them should be at least 700 years older than Sappho's poems, while the latest should be at least 300 years older[30]. Thus, taking into account all the previous assumptions, one could presume that Sappho (c. 615 – 560 BCE) was influenced by the ancient Egyptian love lyrics and had fruitfully assimilated the concomitant influences, filtering them through her poetic genius and her unique talent. History proceeds through mutual interactions of cultures. In the case of Egypt and Greece, this is more than evident, especially since the Saitic and Ptolemaic Periods are examined.

N.B.: Please send offprint requests to Dr. Amanda–Alice Maravelia, e-mail address: **nut_ntrt@otenet.gr**

---

[26] See for instance Dover, K.J.: *Homosexualité grecque*, Paris (La pensée sauvage) 1982; Light, H.: *Sexual Life in Ancient Greece*, London 1994. Cf. also Vrisimitzis, N.A.: *Love, Sex and Marriage in Ancient Greece*, Athens ³1997, pp. 81-5. For Sappho's sexuality see the concomitant chapters in Giebel, M.: *Sappho*, Hamburg (Rowohlt Taschenbuch Verlag) 1980; cf. also those in Weigall: *Sappho of Lesbos ...*, ²1937, chapter IX: "Sappho and her Hetaerae". Concerning homosexuality in ancient Egypt see Manniche, L.: *Sexual Life in Ancient Egypt*, London (KPI) 1987, pp. 22, 24-7, 56-7.

[27] For this topic see Weigall: *Sappho of Lesbos ...*, ²1937, chapter XVI: "Sappho and the Tyrants of Lesbos". Concerning this political system see Berve, H.: *Die Tyrannis bei den Griechen*, **I-II**, München 1967. See also Snell, B.: "Zur Sociologie des Archaischen Griechentums", *Gymnasium*, **65**, 1958, pp. 48-58.

[28] The prominent appearances of women on monuments and literature, as well as their relative freedom and virtual social potential, which were distinctly higher in the ancient Egyptian society than in other contemporary ones, must not be falsely perceived. The gender distinctions existed as a characteristic of the Egyptian social structure, and the women's position was overally lesser than that of men. Hence, the term "matrifocal" should not be understood as "matriarchal", but rather as denoting the high esteem that Egyptians were bestowing towards their charming wifes, sweet mothers, and keen mistresses of their households (*nbwt-prw*), in their roles as such. See, for example, AMORC: *Women of the Nile*, San Jose–CA (*Rosicrucian Egyptian Museum*) 1999. Capel, A.C. & Markoe, G.E. (eds.): *Mistress of the House, Mistress of Heaven. Women in Ancient Egypt*, NY (*Cincinnati Art Museum*) 1996. Desroches-Noblecourt, C.: *La femme au temps des pharaons*, Paris 1986. Fischer, H.G.: *Egyptian Women of the OK ...*, 1989. Hawass, Z.: *Silent Images. Women in Pharaonic Egypt*, NY (H.N. Abrams, Inc) 2000. Lesko, B.: *The Remarkable Women of Ancient Egypt*, Berkeley 1978. Robins, G.: *Women in Ancient Egypt*, London (BMP) 1993. Sadek, A.I.: "Aperçu général sur la femme dans l'Égypte ancienne", *Le Monde Copte*, **16**, 1989, pp. 3-20. Watterson, B.: *Women in Ancient Egypt*, NY (St. Martin's Press) 1991. Wenig, S.: *Die Frau in Ägypten*, Leipzig 1967. For the latest periods see Rowlandson, J.: *Women and Society in Greek and Roman Egypt. A Sourcebook*, UK (Cambridge Univer-sity Press) 1998.

[29] For this topic see Mathieu: *La poésie amoureuse ...*, 1996, pp. 151-9. Cf. also Vernus: *Chants d'amour ...*, 1992, pp. 26-40. Additionally, the social standing of women in the aristocratic society of Mytilênê was much better than that in the later Athenian society, where democracy was true only for Athenian males who were not slaves. See, for instance Kolobova, K.M. & Ozereckaja, E.L.: *Everyday Life in Ancient Greece*, Athens (Papadêmas) ³1989, chapter 3. For this topic, i.e. the noble life and aristocratic ideals of Sappho see Battistini, Y.: *Sapphô. La dixième des Muses*, Paris (Hachette) 1995. See also Weigall: *Sappho of Lesbos ...*, ²1937, chapter VIII: "Sparta and the Dorian and Aeolian Treatment of Women".

[30] The most ancient of them are probably those from *pHarris 500* (early Dyn. XIX); the next older are those from *pTurin 1966* (early Dyn. XX); follow those from *oDeM 1266* and the other various ostraca (Dyn. XIX-XX); the poems of *pChester Beaaty I* seem to be the next later (Dyn. XX); in any case the poem of *sLouvre C100*, is the latest one known (dating probably either from Dyn. XXI or from Dyn. XXV); for the dating of love poems see also Mathieu: *La poésie amoureuse ...*, 1996, pp. 22-3 & references therein, and p. 36, footnote 34. Hence for the love poems of ancient Egypt, most probably, the *terminus a quo* is c. 1300 BCE and the *terminus ad quem* is c. 1000 BCE. In any case the possibility of an even older date for most of the love poems (except for that on *sLouvre C100*), viz the probability that they were initially conceived and primarily written during Dynasty XVIII, the peaceful period of highest cultural achievements is very pronounced. This should mean that most of the extant sources are rather copies of older originals. Anyway, the love poems seem to constitute a pure NK product, which continued to be copied and used during the TIP. This very fact seems true not only because of various linguistic details (see Mathieu: *La poésie amoureuse ...*, 1996, pp. 200-1, passim); also because in many of them the scenes described are reminiscent of the paintings from a multitude of NK tombs (Valley of the Nobles, & c.); for this topic see Maravelia, A.-A.: "Some Aspects of Ancient Egyptian Social Life, by the Study of the Principal Love Poem's Ostraca from Deir 'el-Medineh", *Proceedings of the IAE 8th International Congress* (Hawass, Z. & Brock, L.P., eds.), Cairo (The *AUC* Press) 2001, *forthcoming*.

Fig. 1 Statuette of Hathor, represented as Aphrodite. Graeco–Roman Period, terracotta, h = 26.5 cm, *Musée du Louvre*. From the Hellenistic Period onwards, a great variety of coroplastic creations started to replace the bronze statuettes, and the subsequent themes presented were adapted to the general trends of that period. Hathor was assimilated to the Mediterranean Aphrodite, hence obtaining her attributes. This consists a fine example of the interaction between Egyptian and Greek cultures, the more because it represents a statuette of the matron deity of love/*mrwt*, i.e. Hathor/Aphrodite, evoked both in the LP and S. © *Musée du Louvre*.

Fig. 2 A typical banqueting scene from the tomb of Nakht, priest–astronomer of Amun (Th.T. 52, c. 1400 BCE, Valley of the Nobles, Thebes West), depicting: *On the upper row*: six noble ladies (seated) assisted by a maid–servant (standing); they bear aromatic cones of myrrh fixed on their wigs, together with lotus buds, and they are smelling flowers of lotus and mandragora; a blind harpist is also performing. *On the lower row*: three noblemen are seated, holding sweet–smelling lotus flowers, bearing also cones of myrrh on their heads. They face a table full of offerings: fruits, bread, wine and flowers, mainly lotus and stems of papyri.   © Dr. Amanda–Alice Maravelia.

Fig. 3 Ancient Egyptian decanal and zodiacal constellations, as depicted on the astronomical ceiling (rectangular zodiac) of the pronaos, at the temple of Hathor at Dendera (c. 50 BCE). Sothis (= Isis, *Spdt*) is represented as a recumbent celestial cow inside a divine bark (upper left row), Orion (= Osiris, *S3ḥ*) follows looking back (towards East) at her. Between them the *Dd*–pillar constellation surmounted by the divine Horus falcon bearing the double crown, denoting the New Year's beginning, is represented. The Gemini constellation follows (after a standing astral goddess), represented as the divine pair of primordial divinities Shou and Tefnout.   © Dr. Amanda–Alice Maravelia.

www.ingramcontent.com/pod-product-compliance
Lightning Source LLC
Chambersburg PA
CBHW040903240426
43668CB00024B/2452